WORLD
CLASS
SAILING

OTHER BOOKS BY GARY JOBSON

USYRU Sailing Instructor's Manual
The Racing Edge (with Ted Turner)
The Yachtsman's Pocket Almanac
Gary Jobson's How to Sail
Storm Sailing
Speed Sailing (with Mike Toppa)
Sailing Fundamentals (with the American Sailing Association)

WORLD
CLASS
SAILING

Gary Jobson
and Martin Luray

ADLARD COLES
8 Grafton Street, London W1

Adlard Coles
William Collins Sons & Co. Ltd
8 Grafton Street, London W1X 3LA

First published in Great Britain by
Adlard Coles Ltd 1988
First published in the USA by
Hearst Marine Books 1987

British Library Cataloguing in Publication Data

Jobson, Gary
World class sailing.
1. Yacht racing
I. Title   II. Luray, Martin
797.1'4   GV826.5

ISBN 0-229-11815-1

Printed and bound in Great Britain by
Robert Hartnoll (1985) Ltd, Bodmin

For
Thomas Jobson
and
Will Lee

Foreword by Gary Jobson

*R*acing sailboats is the greatest experience I have ever had. Naturally, the competition on the water and the intense rivalries have been fun, challenging, at times frustrating, but always changing. I believe if you plug away at this sport long enough, you will earn your share of victories. But these victories are backed up by many more defeats.

There is an even larger part to sailing, however, and that is the unique opportunity to meet inspired people who have been successful on and off the water, to sail on the world's greatest yachts and visit some of the world's most exotic ports.

Sailing people are special. They tend to create things that have never been done before and contribute to their fellowman. Many people work hard for success and their ultimate reward is their sailing. That is why this sport is so interesting.

With the boats, speed is always the quest and wind and water are the common denominators, but boats take many forms and I have tried to experience them all. As a tourist, I think it is difficult to really understand people from different parts of the United States and different countries. But thanks to sailing, I've learned more about people throughout the world, ranging across America to Down Under, throughout Europe, South America, and even the Soviet Union. There is no doubt that competitive sailing brings people of the world closer together.

On my frequent lecture tours and sailing trips, the three most frequent questions I am asked are:

1. What is your favorite kind of sailing?
2. What is it like to sail with Ted Turner?
3. What does your wife think of your sailing travels?

I've purposely elected to sail in as many different kinds of boats and regattas as possible. I have gone for the broad range of sailing as opposed to specializing in one particular area of the sport, whether sailing a dinghy single-handed against one hundred boats, match racing a twelve-meter, skipping across the ocean at thirty knots on a megamaran or coordinating the efforts of twenty-six crew on a maxiyacht. It all blends together. After all, you still tack on the headers regardless of how much computer data you have or what kind of boat you are on.

I have a theory that if you stay in this sport long enough, eventually you will sail with everyone. Ted Turner is certainly the most exciting person I have been with on the water and is the one person that has made the sport of sailing interesting to nonsailors. But Ted, like hundreds of others I have crewed for or skippered for, is simply a sailing nut and not really different on the water from anyone else. It is his outside life and business that attract attention to him and the sport of sailing and many of our sailing regattas are recounted here.

I first met Janice Murphy in the spring of 1971. She grew up in Brooklyn and became a nurse. Although not a sailor, she has been with me for both my greatest triumphs and my most disappointing defeats. She tends to travel to regattas about half the time and understands the sport as well as anyone. As for how she puts up with the travel, I guess I'm lucky.

One of the special features of writing this book was working with my friend Marty Luray. Marty is an accomplished sailor himself. He is both a student and a historian of sailing and it was fun working on this project—reflecting on the past, observing the present, and trying to forecast the future of the sport.

Annapolis, Maryland
August 1986

Foreword by
Martin Luray

In the early summer of 1972, as the editor of *Rudder* magazine, I had the good fortune to visit with the late British designer Uffa Fox at his home on the waterfront at Cowes. Uffa Fox was a legend in his own time. Distinguished as a racing sailor in both dinghies and offshore vessels, he was equally at home in the Grand Prix powerboats he had a hand in designing. In England, he was noted for having designed the Flying Fifteen; in the United States not many people knew that the ubiquitous O'Day Daysailer had come off his drawing board. Also off his drawing board had come a little boat that had saved many RAF pilots during the Second World War—a sailing dinghy that could be carried in the belly of a bomber and dropped in the Channel to allow a ditched pilot to sail to friendly shores. Uffa was equally at home with his sailing companion

Prince Philip as he was in his kitchen preparing a whole poached salmon for his friends. He was a good writer; his books about sailing (and how to prepare a salmon) were best sellers in England. A husky, strong redhead in his youth, at seventy-two he was still active as a designer, although he had to curb his physical activity because of heart problems.

I had prepared for the interview by reading all of his books that I could find in England on short notice. When I arrived at the old warehouse he had converted into a home, studio, and workshop, he greeted me in that open way he had and said to the aged housekeeper, "The American journalist is here. See if he'll have a sherry before lunch."

So began the most memorable day in my career as an "American journalist." Our discussions covered not only the world of yacht design but the worlds of politics, literature, and music as well; Uffa was truly what we have come to refer to as a "Renaissance man." At some point I asked him, "What advice would you give a young designer just coming into the business?" And he replied, "I would say to him, 'You won't make much money. But you'll meet a lot of nice people.' "

In retrospect that advice could have applied to me. I was just getting started in writing about sailing. I wasn't making much money at it and probably never would, but Uffa's forecast was correct. I was going to meet a lot of people who were not only nice but interesting as well; the independence that people deeply involved with sailing have seems usually to be coupled with minds that can only be described as extracurricular. They do not think as you and I do.

When Gary Jobson, with whom I had worked on a previous book *(Storm Sailing)*, suggested this one, my mind flashed back to that sunny afternoon in Uffa's house overlooking the harbor at Cowes, and I knew we had the chance to write about the people who frequent Gary's world and mine, and also about the places on this earth that are landmarks in sailors' lives.

Gary grew up sailing and I came to it as an adult, albeit relatively young. I had been a city kid fascinated by the water and by the ocean. It wasn't until we started working on this book that we realized that our early sailing had taken place in the same place, on New Jersey's Barnegat Bay, each going at it from a different direction.

Sailing is very much like that. There are always circles that somehow seem to form and re-form. This book is about sailing at the very top, but it is also about alliances that are made with boats and people and places. Sometimes these alliances are temporary and sometimes they are permanent, but they are part of our memory. And as another "Renaissance man," yachtsman and industrial designer and art critic William Snaith once wrote, "The joys of memory telescope time."

Marblehead, Mass.
August 1986

Acknowledgments

*I*n order to provide some perspective on the places, events, and people described in this book, we dipped into the enormous well of sailing literature for appropriate quotes to help set scenes or give the reader a taste of yachting history. Thanks are due, therefore, to the following:

Sail magazine for permission to quote from articles by John McNamara, Jeff Spranger, Roger Vaughan, Norris Hoyt, and Robby Robinson.

Sports Illustrated for the quotes from Coles Phinizy's article (July 4, 1977) "Staging a Battle Royal on the Briny." Copyright © 1977 by Time, Inc.

The New York Times for the excerpts from William Wallace's article (July 30, 1977) "Patience of Jobson. . . ." Copyright © 1977 by The New York Times Company. Reprinted by permission.

Julius Wilensky for permission to use material from the fourth edition (1971) of his *Guide to Long Island Sound*. *Waterway Guide* for the quotes from Walter Cronkite's Introduction to the 1986 edition of this invaluable publication.

Joseph Howard Cooper for permission to excerpt a portion of his description of the Larchmont Yacht Club in his book *Land's End, Water's Edge*.

International Marine Publishing Company, and particularly Roger Taylor, for the use of quotes from *John Alden and His Yacht*. Designs by Robert W. Carrick and Richard Henderson.

L. Francis Herreshoff's portrait of Captain Charley Barr first appeared in *Rudder* magazine and most recently in *An L. Francis Herreshoff Reader,* published by International Marine Publishing Company.

W. W. Norton and Co., Inc., and Eric Swenson for permission to quote from *Yacht Designing and Planning* by Howard Chappelle.

Bill Robinson for allowing us to excerpt from the chapter "Racing to Bermuda" in his book *The Sailing Life*.

Carleton Mitchell for permission to quote from his evocative essays on cruising on the Chesapeake in *The Winds Call*. Both books were published by Charles Scribner's Sons.

Also profound thanks to Kathy Thompson who kept the Annapolis end of things on track. Paul Larsen's initial impetus brought the book into being. And at Hearst Marine, a special acknowledgment for three who kept the faith: Sarah Borden, John Whiting, and Connie Roosevelt, whose patience and editorial perception made life under deadline pressures infinitely more bearable.

CONTENTS

INTRODUCTION

For twenty years I have been averaging between 120 and 160 days a year on the water, racing sailboats. I first began racing in 1957 when at the age of seven I crewed on a ten-foot pram on the Toms River in New Jersey. At seventeen I decided that sailing would be my sport. To this day, I'm not sure whether I made the decision because my family had always been involved with sailing and racing on Barnegat Bay or because I was out to prove myself as a racer; doing well on the racecourse did not, in fact, come easily until I was seventeen.

Since those first days on the pram the intervening years seemed to have gone by at breakneck speed, with some very dramatic changes taking place in the sport.

Just thirty years ago, most boats were made of wood, with fiberglass on the verge of being used as a boatbuilding material. Synthetics, Dacron and nylon were being established as the materials out of which sails were made. One-design racing was in its heyday—flourishing all over the United States. Ocean racing was closer to cruising than the technologically advanced Grand Prix style we know today.

Within a few years, the fiberglass revolution turned sailing into a sport that many more people were able to afford; boats lasted longer and were much more easily maintained. High-tech advances moved into the racing scene almost faster than the sport could absorb them. A new, enormously strong synthetic fiber, Kevlar, found its way into sailmaking and boatbuilding, providing a strength-to-weight ratio hitherto unforeseen. Ultralight Mylar made ultralight sails for ultralight boats; suddenly ULDB's (ultralight displacement boats) were the thing. Exotic construction—fiberglass sandwiches with cores of space-age–named materials such as Nomex and Airex—is part of the new revolution that began with fiberglass and seems to have no perceivable end.

Meantime, as I grew into the sport, it changed its complexion and its texture. One-design racing (in boats all built to the same specifications) dropped off—most dramatically over the past few years. A new form of racing that tends to equalize boats and crews—Performance Handicap Racing Fleet (PHRF)—has become popular as sailors move away from dinghies into larger boats. The Grand Prix racing circuit of top-of-the-line racing boats increased in competitiveness, innovation, and expense but no longer has the numbers that it once did; fewer boats are being built and campaigned at a high level. In 1986, for example, only fifty-two yachts raced in the most important showpiece in the racing

round robin—the Southern Ocean Racing Circuit
(SORC)—compared with a fleet of 140 in 1973. There
are fewer competitors perhaps because to win on the
Grand Prix circuit today, you better have a custom designed yacht. At times production boats may win an
event, but never on a consistent basis.

The America's Cup, long regarded as the pinnacle of
amateur yacht racing, has changed from a summer activity that occupied a relative handful of old-line
yachtsmen on Long Island Sound and Newport every
few years to a full-time profession for sailors, boatbuilders, designers, sailmakers, fundraisers, and public-
relations people in at least seven countries this year.
The ages of the skippers and the crews has decreased
also; this is no longer a sport participated in only by
wealthy gentlemen. In the 1930s all of the America's
Cup skippers were in their fifties. In the 1960s all of
the skippers were in their forties. In the 1970s, the top
helmsmen were in their thirties. Now, in the 1980s,
sailors in their mid twenties are emerging as the leading twelve-meter helmsmen. In the 1986 twelve-meter
World Championships, held off Fremantle, Australia,
the skipper of the winning *Australia III* was twenty-
six. The second-place finisher was twenty-four. An international circuit of very good young sailors has developed in response to the needs of those racing the big
maxiboats (over eighty feet) and the twelves.

Prior to the Second World War, very few yacht clubs
in the United States had junior sailing programs. But
following World War II, perhaps because of the baby-
boom generation, junior sailing programs popped up
by the hundreds at yacht clubs around the country. My
first eight years of sailing was as a member of the junior program at the Beachwood Yacht Club on Bar-

negat Bay at Toms River, N.J. I raced constantly, and occasionally I sailed with my father on a variety of catboats and sloops he owned.

When I first began racing, some of America's best sailors—Cornelius Shields, Ted Wells, Arthur Knapp, and Rod Stephens—were studying the sport very carefully and then telling us in their books how to improve. They searched hard for clever ways to gain an edge over their opponents and kept talking and writing about what they had discovered in tactics that might help the average club racer. Their openness encouraged others to enter the sport of sailing. Unfortunately, this trend has stopped; many of America's best sailors have become highly secretive in their quest to excel.

We did a lot of reading in those days to understand how the masters did it. Arthur Knapp's classic *Race Your Boat Right* was first published in 1952 and has been reissued many times since; it remains a very useful book. In 1964 Cornelius Shields published *Racing with the Masters,* another important work. We read *Scientific Sailboat Racing* by Ted Wells (1950) and *Yacht Racing: The Aerodynamics of Sails* by Manfred Curry (1948). We tried to understand *Sailing Theory and Practice* by C. A. Marchaj (1962) and were guided by Dr. Stewart Walker's first book *The Techniques of Small Boat Racing,* published in 1966.

When it came to periodicals, the one publication that spoke directly to racers in the early 1960s was a magazine called *One Design,* later *One Design and Offshore Racing,* then *Yacht Racing,* next *Yacht Racing/Cruising,* and now *Sailing World.* The publication stayed with us as we moved to larger boats; a whole generation grew up with this important periodical.

We had our heroes, too—men such as George O'Day, an Olympic racer and boat designer; Bus Mosbacher;

and Bob Bavier. All these men helped the United States successfully defend the America's Cup. They were men totally dedicated to sailboat racing; they were our role models, as were others who became totally immersed in the sailing industry, such as sailmaker and racer Lowell North; sailmaker, yacht designer and America's Cup helmsman Ted Hood; and boatbuilder and racer Buddy Melges.

As the sport changed along with other professed amateur sports such as skiing, we changed, too. Many of us became professionals in a sport that once had condemned professionalism as not sporting. Sailing's impact on my life over the past twenty years has been profound—highs and lows of victories and defeats, sailing with peers and mentors in places and waters that became as familiar as the view out of my back door in Annapolis. And learning, always learning, from people of prominence and wisdom and wealth who invited me on their boats to do a job for them—to train a crew or sail their vessels almost as if we were in the old days, when yachtsmen had sailing masters to help run their vessels. Today, however, the mode is different: There is a cross-pollination in which showing how to get the best out of a boat and crew is swapped for some inkling of how to get the best out of life, as they know it.

That is what these chapters are about, a path from where we started to where we are and where we ought to be in this sport. They tell of what we learned from competition and commuting to work on the water from Chesapeake Bay to the China Sea, the boats we sailed, and the sometimes unorthodox but always interesting men who owned or sailed them. Rod Stephens, who taught us how to rig a boat right and sail it well, once wrote, "There is no end to learning." And there isn't.

1

THIS CHANGING SPORT

*I*n 1966, the Barnegat Bay Racing Association named me as the Outstanding Junior Sailor of the Year. Although I had not won any major championships, most of the time I was close to the front. But most important, unlike many sailors on the bay, I was sailing full time while going to school. I raced in the fall, sailed with the Frostbite fleet every winter weekend, and resumed racing in the spring. I was sixteen then, and I had decided that whenever a sailing oportunity came along I would be ready. So I crewed on auxiliaries in Barnegat Bay, raced E-Scows with one of the top amateurs, Sam Merrick; and skippered Penguins on the East Coast from the Chesapeake Bay to Long Island Sound on the winter circuit.

My mentor in those days was a hot Penguin sailor named Dick Curry, for whom I crewed a great deal.

Curry encouraged me to stay with the sport and introduced me to the idea of trying to enroll in the New York Maritime College, which had a strong sailing team and an impressive coach, Graham Hall, who had won six straight national titles as the coach of the U.S. Naval Academy sailing team and two others at New York Maritime.

Being on the winter racing circuit meant going to every regatta we could possibly make. We would load up Curry's Volkswagen with one Penguin on top and another in a trailer. The Penguin circuit in those days (late 1950s through the early 1970s) offered perhaps one of the best organized and most competitive fleets in the country. On any given weekend, between forty and eighty boats would converge on the host yacht club. The races were short. Sometimes we would have as many as ten races in a two-day period. It was a learning time for me; when I arrived at New York Maritime I had a solid foundation in making a boat go fast and was well rounded as both helmsman and crewman.

In retrospect it was the age of innocence. We were all amateurs, especially in college, competing for the fun of it. The idea of making money out of sailing, or racing, was so farfetched as to be unheard of. The thought that a regatta might be commercially sponsored or a boat backed financially simply never occurred to anyone. Purity reigned in organized sailing both here and aboard, as it did in the Olympic world. Rich men, therefore, raced the big boats and wrote personal checks to finance the twelve-meter yachts that were to defend the America's Cup. (As recently as 1980, the funds for the two American defenders were privately raised.)

Today I still am on the water most of the year, but

the difference is profound. Today, I and many others in the sport are sailing as professionals; although we are not getting paid to race, we are making a living thanks to the sport. And the regattas we race in as well as the boats we race on may have commercial backing. Sail racing along with other formerly amateur sports has become big business, although as a TV viewing sport it lags far behind. Is this trend necessarily bad, recognizing that sailing is only recently taking its place in the ranks of sports that have "gone commercial"? Let's examine two sides of this sailing business.

PROFESSIONALISM:
You Play Like a Pro

"You play like a pro." With these words you give the highest compliment to a young ballplayer. But in sailing, the word "professional" has negative connotations. *The American Heritage Dictionary* defines professionalism as "having great skill or experience in a particular field or activity." But in the sailing world, people are afraid to say they are professionals and are astounded when their name is linked with the word even though they are employed in the marine industry at the same time that they crew on racing yachts.

What is professionalism as it applies to "amateur" sports? Rule 26 of the governing rules of the Olympic Games states under eligibility for participation: "A competitor must not be a professional athlete in any sport" or "have allowed his person, name, picture, or sports performance to be used for advertising" or "have acted as a professional coach or trainer in any sport.''

It's unrealistic and hypocritical to think that an athlete can abide by these rules. Almost every Olympic athlete, whether in yachting or other events, violates each of those codes. It is legal, for instance, to have your name or picture in an advertisement as long as a token donation is sent to the U.S. Olympic Committee (USOC) along with a sample of the advertisement. What this does, of course, is allow the USOC to make believe that all is well in the amateur ranks. Yet a runner such as Carl Lewis earned more than a million dollars in the year before the last Olympic Games, while running champion Edwin Moses is paid handsomely for personal appearances; their status, logically, is that of professional.

A tug-of-war between amateur and professional sailors has become very evident in the past few years and is bound to become more of a conflict as the sport becomes more and more commercially oriented. Most of the owners of top ocean-racing yachts employ two persons. One organizes the boat, its crew, and the campaign. The other person is known as the sailing master, or "the professional on the boat" and performs as a member of the crew. The eligibility committee of the U.S. Yacht Racing Union has ruled that this is perfectly acceptable as long as the person is not paid to race. (But what else do the boat and, ergo, the "professionals" do?)

What is a professional? We decry the Eastern Bloc attitude toward keeping top athletes as full-time professionals. Yet for the last Olympic trials two U.S. Navy officers were assigned to train for the Olympics. The U.S. government was paying the salaries of these sailors while they trained.

In the meantime, while the debate goes on, the

America's Cup competition has thrown the conflict over professionalism into a cocked hat. The America's Cup used to be the sport of wealthy gentlemen who, early on, hired crews for their giant J-boats, then later convinced husky young college kids and working sailors to spend a summer, without pay, racing twelves for the glory of it. It may have been glorious then, but now some two hundred people have been sailing on twelve-meters as a full-time occupation, some for more than four years.

And sailors, whether they are "amateur" or not, seem to be good business themselves as the purveyors of nonmarine products. Twelve-meter skipper Dennis Conner and onetime twelve-meter helmsman and sail-maker Ted Hood promote Rolex watches. Ted Turner has appeared in ads for DHL delivery service and Hathaway shirts. Designer Bruce Nelson has turned up in AMC jeep ads, and Dewar's Scotch had me sitting in a bathtub. None of us would have appeared at all if not for sailing.

Still, with all the money around, one boundary has not been crossed, and that may help redefine the "amateur" yachtsman of today. In some sports, the line is drawn when the athlete accepts prize money or a "bonus" for winning. That has yet to happen in sailing, and for the moment we are saved.

COMMERCIALISM:
What's in a Name?

In yacht racing, the answer to that question now is money. Offshore racing in special events has succumbed to sponsorship of boats and, as time passes, more and more regattas are going the same way. Big companies have discovered that putting up the money to sponsor a boat or a regatta is an effective way to get institutional "brand name" advertising. On a world-scale event, such as the Whitbread Round-the-World Race, the name of your boat (i.e., the name of your company) is in front of the public every day. And, obviously, if you sponsor a regatta, you get a free plug in the coverage and write-up of the race results. Pro tennis and pro golf (for "regattas," substitute "matches") have been involved with this for years, with backers such as Volvo and Virginia Slims. But for American sailing, it has been a long time in coming—the long-established ideal of the pure yachtsman dying hard.

The Europeans did it first. In fact, it was the British, despite the myth of amateur purity that clings to Britain, who saw the possibilities of international reknown in a single-handed race across the Atlantic from Plymouth, England, to Newport, R.I. It was an event that had its origin in a proposal by British yachtsman and World War II hero H. G. (Blondie) Hasler that there be a solo transatlantic race in 1960. The idea was taken up by four English sailors, including Sir Francis Chichester, and one French sailor. The *London Observer* decided to back it, the race became known as the *Observer* Single-handed Transatlantic Race (OSTAR) and that may have been the beginning of commercialism in yacht racing as we know it today.

The OSTAR still continues, of course, as it has since 1960. The four entrants in that year grew to ninety-one official starters from 16 countries in 1984. And what also grew right along with the event was commercial sponsorship of individual boats. Need dictated that move; to enter OSTAR took money that very few single individuals had. The result was a race for corporate sponsorship, with organizations such as Club Méditerranée backing a 236-foot four-masted vessel that sported four jibs. (The rules no longer allow this; sixty feet overall is the maximum length.) But the British and the French now saw their way clear in other events to look for commercial sponsorship. And so you had a monster trimaran called *British Oxygen* in the Round Britain Race in 1973. Corporate sponsorship also brought small embarrassments. When British singlehander Clare Francis obtained backing from James Robertson & Sons, a British candy manufacturer, for her 1976 entry, she named the boat *Robertson's Golly* for one of the company's well-known products. Golly, it turned out, was short for golliwog, a jigging blackamoor that was the company's logo and hardly suitable for an American audience.

Corporate sponsorship since then has burgeoned to the extent that of the fifteen boats in the 1986 Whitbread Round the World Race, ten carried the names of their commercial underwriters. Sometimes the mix of corporate-backed and noncorporate boats makes for an interesting sidelight. In the 1983 Whitbread, the well-named *Flyer,* built, paid for, and sailed by the Dutch yachtsman Cornelius van Reischoten, dueled its way around the world with *Ceramco New Zealand,* a maxi-vessel built and paid for by a New Zealand ceramics manufacturer. (*Flyer* won.)

There is no end in sight to this sponsorship phenomenon—companies feel that sailors reflect an authentic, vicarious "man against the sea" image. They are beginning to underwrite regattas because they feel that such an image honestly encourages people to think highly of their company or product. Currently Anheuser-Busch, Stroh's, Dewar's Scotch, Swarovski Crystal, Mumms, Volvo Penta, De Beers, and Ciba-Geigy are in the game. So are General Motors, Ford, Chrysler, MCI, and Pacific Telesis.

The jury still is out on whether commercial sponsorship hurts or helps the sport of sailing. Some cling to the ideal of pure sport, "untainted" by boats named *Skopbank of Finland* or *UBS Switzerland* (a large Swiss conglomerate). Commercial sponsorship of boats and regattas can provide the financial wherewithal and corporate backup to run and publicize the event properly and therefore keep sailing in the public eye.

The public eye, of course, does its seeing through the picture tube, and that is where sailing is far behind other sports; it is just beginning to capture an audience through television.

SAILING ON TELEVISION:
Eye, There's the Rub

The time seems ripe for sailboat racing finally to break through on television. The clues are there—the use of elegant modern racing craft in TV commercials showing the glamour (and the hard work) of it all. Macho sport. Camaraderie among hard-bitten but handsome men in the throes of competition. There was daily live and tape coverage of the America's Cup races in 1983, but since then no recognition of sailboat racing as a sport to be reckoned with or covered on TV. Even the Olympic yachting events didn't really make it, despite the United States' clean sweep (three golds and four silvers out of seven classes) at Long Beach. Unfortunately, only seventeen minutes of sailing made it on ABC during the Olympic Games in 1984.

The networks have lacked commitment to a sport they deem logistically and technically difficult to cover despite apparent interest by the American audience, sailing being more ubiquitous than the networks realize, with over a hundred thousand new participants each year. Sailboat racing doesn't even seem to fit into the Saturday and Sunday afternoon TV sports ghettos with their oddball coverage of triathlons and competitive rock climbing.

Sports columnist Red Smith is said to have compared viewing the America's Cup with "watching grass grow." Unfortunately, he wasn't up close enough to hear the shouts of crewmen at work as they changed jibs quicker than you could say *The New York Times,* or watched the coordinated ballet of flawlessly raising a spinnaker under intense pressure.

It's true that watching a fleet racing in light air isn't the stuff that will set the TV viewer on fire. But more often than not, the excitement is there. The 1986 Twelve-Meter Worlds, held in Fremantle, Australia, was billed as the testing ground for the 1987 America's Cup. When the Fremantle Doctor—the local afternoon blow that averages twenty to twenty-five knots—hit the multimillion-dollar fleet of expensive boats, hardware, and people, four boats were dismasted, and seven crewmen on six different boats were washed overboard. There were times when fourteen of the twelves— all averaging sixty-five feet—would round the windward mark in twenty-five knots of breeze within ninety seconds of each other. Elegance and potential destruction all in the same breath, and there was no question about the excitement that was engendered among the TV viewers on Australia's Channel 9.

Channel 9, in fact, had little trouble with making the commitment to cover the Worlds—of prime interest in a country that had taken the unprecedented step of capturing the America's Cup in 1983 and saw no reason why it shouldn't stay there in 1987. Sailing is a major sport along Australia's coasts; it exports as many top crewman and professional skippers to the world sailing community as it does wool for the sweaters of America. Channel 9 used six cameras: two mounted on helicopters to show the action from the air, and four cameras on the water.

The most dramatic moments on television, however, were not the hardships the boats faced but the changes in the lead, which happened in every race and often on different legs of the course. Watching the live coverage of two boats racing side by side was as fascinating and as breathtaking in its beauty as seeing two Thoroughbreds racing neck and neck for the wire. Sometimes one boat would point higher and the other would foot faster, but the unfolding drama from mark to mark was better than watching a football team slowly catch up with its opponents by making perfect plays. Red Smith would have loved it.

It's obvious that Australian television is pointing the way, and their next step probably will be to put mini-cameras aboard the boats. Radio-controlled cameras that weigh only eight pounds could be tucked almost anywhere. Can you imagine the impact on a viewer of the 1983 America's Cup if during the seventh race there had been a camera on board each of the yachts to focus on the faces of the crews and the skippers and hear what they were saying during those decisive moments on the fifth leg of the course when *Australia II* regained the lead?

The danger of match racing on television is the same as that of matchups in any sport: The boats, like teams or players, have to be even in ability to start with so the viewer will anticipate a close event. Evenly matched boats force lots of maneuvering and tacking, crew work becomes important, mistakes and gear failures become significant. The lead can keep changing, and the result may not be known until the first boat crosses the finish line, perhaps less than a second ahead of its opponent. This was what happened in race after race of the Twelve-Meter Worlds. At least three times during the championships, any of four boats had a chance of winning within the last mile before the finish.

TV coverage of sailing raises the question of whether sailors are equipped to be media stars. Great basketball, baseball, and football players learn to live with the press at an early age, but sailors are sheltered. They perform far from shore without the benefit of screaming crowds. In place of the locker-room interview, there are dock-side interviews, and the crews and their skippers have to learn how to deal with prying cameras as well as story-hungry reporters. An honest, sympathetic interview begets loyal audiences and attracts new sponsors.

Ted Turner, through deed and word and force of a quixotic personality, probably has done more than anyone else to awaken Americans to the sport of sail-boat racing, and the Turner network, WTBS, covered the sailing events of the Goodwill Games from Tallinn, Estonia. ESPN is set to cover the America's Cup trials and challenge from Australia more fully than any other television network in the history of the America's Cup.

ESPN first had to educate its viewers on what the America's Cup was all about and prove to them that

twelve-meter racing really is a bona fide form of athletic competition. During the summer of 1986, each of
the America's Cup films from 1958 to the present was
shown. Additional shows focused on each American
challenge syndicate for 1987 as well as the Aussie defenders. ESPN also produced short spots (for use during the actual coverage) about equipment that might
fail, profiles of the crews, match-racing tactics, technology behind the designs, and the drama of the competition on water and on land.

To make television work, producers will have to
combine great action, a balance of aerial and water-level
photography, and good close-ups of the crews in action accompanied by eavesdropping audio that will give
a perspective of what it's like to be part of a top-flight
racing crew. They'll have to experiment with new forms
of technology to make coverage exciting. But television is on its way, perhaps helping the sport toward
its ultimate level.

AMATEUR RACING:
The Way We Were,
the Way We Are

We are sitting in a lounge in Auckland, New Zealand,
waiting for our protest to be heard, this after the first
day of racing at the Royal New Zealand Yacht Squadron's Citizen's Cup. The event pits ten of the world's
top match-racing skippers against each other, and in-

terestingly enough, each skipper is now involved in a protest after the first three races. It's now six o'clock in the evening, and the club has arranged two juries to hear the protests at hearings that probably will stretch until 1:00 A.M. Ten boats had spent four hours racing on the water followed by seven hours of protests in a sterile committee room.

The protest committee obviously has been through this before. A large coffeepot is available with hot coffee for the protesters, who sat in the lounge much like patients waiting to see a dentist. The room, with its sparse furniture and worn sailing magazines, is not unlike that of a medical waiting room. In fact, the competitors, like patients, have little to say to each other except to those who favor the same side. To them, the Arab philosophy "the enemy of thy enemy is thy friend" seemed to apply as they speak in hushed tones.

In the other room are the judges, theoretically wise men all, who know the sport and its rules well and who are completely qualified to hear the protests and issue rulings. But they and the protesters know that the best judge of all is not human but a videocamera. Naturally, all the skippers are anxious to see what the situation actually looked like, as transmitted to the videotape recorder. But the video machine is not working, and the burden is on the humans running the hearings.

Counting on their wisdom are ten prominent world-class yachtsmen, seven of whom will be skippers at the 1987 America's Cup trials. Of the other three, besides myself, two are Olympic gold medalists. Certainly this group includes the world's best, and yet, one has to ask, why are they in the protest room? It had been windy, certainly, gusting up to thirty-five knots. It also was the first day of the regatta, and emotions may have been charged up a little higher than normal.

But that doesn't seem to be the answer. In the lounge I am sitting next to Iain Murray, who is a six-time world champion in Australian eighteens. In 1984, he won the Etchells World Championships, skippered *Advance* of Australia in the 1983 America's Cup challenge, and will be skippering a new Australian twelve-meter named *Kookaburra* in the 1987 events. Murray had won two of his three races that day. Later, after the protests are heard, he ends up with a zero-and-three record. How could such a clever skipper end up in such an unfortunate mess?

The answer, unfortunately, seems to be that protests have become a way of life in the racing community, signifying one of the important changes in amateur racing. When I grew up sailing on Barnegat Bay, it was generally felt that protests were unthinkable unless the violation was blatant. You weren't involved in a protest if you didn't need to be. One great sailor on the bay had won many championships, but his record was marred by the nickname "The Great Protester" because he was continually in the jury room. The nickname lingers today, three decades later.

In collegiate sailing I learned my lesson about protests. During the first two years of racing, I found that I often lost regattas thanks to being involved in protests, some of which I won and some of which I lost. The average, I discovered, is about fifty-fifty for any sailor. So the best percentage is not to get into a protest at all.

Apparently, however, protesting has become an integral part of racing, because the stakes have become so much higher among the quasi-professional skippers who have taken over the top levels of the sport. The

protest is used as a technique to unsettle another skipper or at least get the red protest flag up for a minor
infringement during the starting maneuvers. Then, if
you lose the race, you have something to fall back on.
In 1983 *Australia II* flew a protest flag in the last three
races but never filed, since she crossed the line first.

For some, a racing day without protests is unthinkable. In a full summer of match racing between Dennis
Conner and Tom Blackaller during the 1983 America's
Cup trials, neither made it through a full day of racing
without at least one protest.

Other examples abound. The great Irish match racing skipper Harold Cudmore, who will be running the
British twelve-meter entry in 1987, has gained a reputation for being in more protests per race than any other
skipper in the world. The New Zealand regatta is no
exception; he is in the lounge with the rest of us, and
it is not the first time I have seen him in the hearing
room. In 1985, a protest I lost to Cudmore cost me the
Liberty Cup.

Protests breed rivalry and emotions. Today, in an
effort to get back at Cudmore, I made a point of sailing
over to the press boat and announcing that I was going
to do something no one had done before: finish the
race ahead of Cudmore without getting into a protest.
It was a tough challenge. We circled wildly at the start,
and although I usually am aggressive trying to get an
advantage, my major goal was to stay clear and go in
for an even start to avoid a protest situation.

I drew a sigh of relief when we crossed the starting
line against Cudmore with no red flags flying. As it
turned out, we established a strong ten-boat-length lead
thanks to a favorable wind shift and never were chal-
lenged again in the race.

Despite the preponderance of protests in yacht racing

these days, there are ways of putting a damper on them. The responsibility for protests does not lie with the competitor alone. It also involves the race committee and the jury. Any major championship would do well to include a videotape system, particularly at starts and mark roundings. Many light-displacement boats, including modern ocean racers, maneuver very quickly; therefore, shorter starting sequences can help decrease the number of protests.

Having highly qualified judges at regattas is essential. And it is important for race organizers to keep the course clear of congested areas and other fleets. Most protests seem to happen in choppy waters; starting lines and courses should be a little bit longer.

Still, the significance of the plethora of protests in today's racing is that it helps tell us what the sport has come to in terms of competition and the people competing. It's revealing to trace the changes in ocean racing over the past twenty years.

Twenty years ago, ocean racing was more like performance cruising than the hard-nut competition we have today. Boats raced from one point to another, but the crews shortened sails at night and believed in the benefits of some comforts while they raced. Ted Turner, in fifteen years of racing aboard his boats such as *American Eagle, Lightning, Vamp X,* and *Tenacious,* changed all of that and led racing out of the performance-cruising era into the Grand Prix Age.

Turner believed in racing a boat full time on a long-distance race, not only during the day. He raced to the maximum, holding sails to the last moment before shortening them down. He flew spinnakers in heavy air when nobody else would. He made sure that the crew sat on the windward rail all the time. And as he did it, he had experienced crew around him who decided that old-fashioned bulwarks really were uncomfortable for sitting on the rail and probably were unnecessary. The next boat would have the bulwark cut down and probably had the minimum furniture below to save weight. But it was Turner's racing style that began to influence the course of the sport. He was doing something right; between 1966 and 1980, he was largely unbeatable.

His influence had an effect on his waterborne competitors such as Ted Hood and Lowell North, who also were servicing him with sails. At the same time, designers and other skippers of top-flight racing boats were picking up the notion that boats could be much faster than they were through the innovative use of lightweight but strong materials. Everyone began striving in a scientific way to develop boat speed, learning not only from winning IOR (International Offshore Rule) designs but from developments in twelve-meter yachts as well.

It also became obvious that full-time racing meant experienced, dedicated crews, giving birth to a breed of sailor (like myself) who lives to sail and who sails to live. Advances in technology changed boats into full-time racers that roam the world in search of competition. And as there was little room for part-time sailors on these "Grand Prix" boats, crews have become more or less permanent and extremely good at what they do best, which is sail, because that is all they do. They are the modern versions of the sailors who manned the square-riggers and the grain clippers of the nineteenth century; their shore time is limited, and they have chosen a seagoing life.

It's instructive to understand how a Grand Prix racer

functions and the part a professional like myself plays in the mix of crew, owner, and boat.

Most Grand Prix yachts have a coordinator like myself with the task of organizing the boat's racing campaign, with a monthly retainer to help the owner enter regattas, advise him on what races to enter, recruit the crew, and handle logistics, all of which is time-consuming.

A typical Grand Prix racer's crew probably will be composed of the following members: Three are involved in sailmaking (two from the sail loft supplying the boat's sails, and one from a sail loft the owner is considering). One is from the office of the naval architect who designed the boat. Several will be from equipment manufacturers, and they will be good sailors. One of the crew may be from the yard that built the boat. Then you have the professional on board and his mate or assistants, all of whom are full-time paid hands. The remainder of the crew is apt to be composed of two or three sailors who live out of seabags, traveling from one regatta to another. Watch captains, navigators, and trimmers are the most difficult to sign on. With them, you have the burden of proof that your boat is worthy of their experience and presence. There is no room, obviously, in this sort of crew, for someone who commutes to Wall Street, as there was in the past.

Eventually the owner may befriend the professionals, and the arrangement works because the boat is more competitive.

ULTIMATE SAILING:
The Ultimate Circuit

For me, no matter what kind of event I am racing in, whether it be *Yachting*'s PHRF Race Week, the America's Cup, the Bermuda Race, or one of the match-race regattas throughout the world, I find that I attack it with the same competitive instincts. Because many sailors like me sail in these types of events, the general level of competition has risen dramatically in recent years. But there has been growing strength to separate the professional sailor who sails a majority of the time from the weekend sailor. The people who sail the most get better at the game. This is no different from tennis, golf, or any other activity. But unlike other sports, the full-time sailor and the weekender share the same forum. Eventually we may see a split in the two groups. Perhaps the full-time sailors will race in a circuit of their own.

And that may be the direction sailboat racing will finally take—an ultimate circuit for those who spend all their time racing with no other commitments, devoting their lives to trying to be the best there is afloat. In this professional Grand Prix Ocean Racing Circuit, the boats and crews will move around the world to sponsored international regattas. As the premium will be on speed, the boats will be designed to go much faster than they do now, at least fifteen knots upwind. They are currently designed to rate well under the International Offshore Rule (IOR). This is a method of handicapping boats based on their length, breadth, displacement (weight), sail area, and other factors. The boat is then given a rating that signifies which class she may race in, from "A" (biggest) to "E" (smallest). The function of the IOR is to equalize boats, but, critics say, because designers have found loopholes in the rule, some boats are more equal than others.

In the ultimate circuit, boats will be designed and built for speed. Once that threshold is crossed, leading to a kind of ocean-racing one-design class that will compete without handicap rules, then the Grand Prix Circuit, with top prize money waiting at the finish lines, will become a reality.

Such a round-the-world circuit, of two years' duration, would take the burden off the lower racing echelons, who would no longer have to worry about being outclassed. The realities of modern-day offshore racing would be faced: Everyone on the racing scene would have a place to go. The full-time crews would have their place. The part-time racers would cling to the club circuits. Prize money would be made up front in the Grand Prix world, and glory would be theirs who continue to compete in the amateur ranks. And who's to say that the kids competing in Penguins in Marblehead Harbor, like the kids playing half-court basketball in Brooklyn, won't have eyes on the pros. The ultimate circuit will be the place to go, if they want to.

2

REGATTAS: BLOOD SPORT ON THE HIGH SEAS

*T*he great yacht designer L. Francis Herreshoff, as quick with the acid pen as he was with a set of drawing tools, never was one to hide his pet peeves. One of them was ocean racing, which he considered unfit for gentlemen. As he wrote in *The Common Sense of Yacht Design,* "Some yachtsmen seem to think the whole object of sailing is to beat a brother yachtsman . . . they sail around courses perhaps at a rate of five miles an hour, and if they win, they consider themselves great sailors."

L. Francis delighted in speed, but not necessarily in competition with others, even though he and his father, Nathaniel Herreshoff, had produced their share of winners. "I must confess that I get a greater thrill out of sailing fast than winning a race and care little for the luffing, backwinding, and crowding at the marks,"

L. Francis Herreshoff wrote. "That sort of business may be all right for sea lawyers and sadists . . . whose only thrill in racing is to spoil the other fellow's chances or rule him out on a technicality." A confirmed small-boat sailor, Captain Francis felt venomous about big ocean racers and how they were manned, "composed mostly of gigolo yacht jockeys; that is, they are kept by the owner to sail for him."

But for all of his cantankerousness about racing, L. Francis Herreshoff's output included the fastest of the R-class boats, *Yankee* and *Live Yankee;* the fastest M-class racer, *Istalena;* and what was described as the most advanced of the 1930 America's Cup defenders, the J-boat *Whirlwind.* Probably more famous in the postwar decades is the seventy-two-foot ketch *Ticonderoga,* in her time the fastest vessel afloat in the Caribbean and holder of many passage records.

So it appears that Captain Francis, despite protestations to the contrary, was intrigued enough by the racing world to design for it during his heyday and even to accept a commission to get into the America's Cup. The lure of the regatta was on him; L. Francis couldn't resist a good set-to, especially if it was match racing. Anyone who has sailed on one of his smaller boats, such as the Rozinante or his father's Alerion, knows how seakindliness, speed, and a happy helm can be successfully combined. And anyone who has had the good fortune to sail on *Big Ti* in her prime knows the sublime thrill of charging through seas at speed, rail under, all sails set and trimmed, the vessel undaunted by anything the ocean can think of.

When L. Francis died in Marblehead, Mass., in 1972 at eighty-two, the modern era of racing was just introducing itself; he could see the mix of wood and fiberglass boats in Marblehead Harbor from the balcony of his house ("The Castle")—some out-and-out racing boats, some cruising vessels, and some "racer-cruisers," another favorite Herreshoff target.

What would he have thought of the new era in yachting that he was not to be part of? There had been long-distance ocean races that spanned the Atlantic and its parts all through his years. There had been local regattas before the turn of the century, some of which he had accompanied his father to view. There had been America's Cup regattas in pilot schooners, cutters, 130-foot J-boats with thirty-two in crew and finally (after World War II) in twelve-meter yachts with eleven in crew. Four of these Cup defenses had occurred during the latter part of his life.

But during the next two and a half decades, Herreshoff would have been startled but probably not surprised to see the America's Cup leap in three-year increments from million-dollar syndicate investments to multimillion-dollar backing efforts, from one-boat-one-syndicate to multiboats per backer, from one challenge per Cup from the British or the Australians to a literal foreign invasion. And finally, the departure of the Auld Mug away from America to the brash western frontier of Australia and another quantum jump in expense and marine technology.

And ocean racing, which he disliked because of the slowness of the yachts and the wealth of the owners and their crews of "gigolo yacht jockeys," also has leaped into a round-the-world racing circuit for big yachts and professional crews, but boat speeds have increased only four or five knots. The onset of a match-racing circuit might have suited him more, but the idea of its being global would take some getting used to

(Herreshoff never ventured any farther from Marble-head than he had to).

That a few sailors dedicated to racing sailboats could participate in all of these events, and more, probably would be an alien idea to him. But that is what has happened: The top regattas have become assemblies of boats, crews, and skippers, most of whom have met at previous events. Only the venue changes: Harbors, waters, the ocean, and the weather are different each time. Each regatta has its style, each place its own characteristics. The racing is hard-nosed, with crews who know their jobs; in match racing, tactics and smarts count heavily. What follows is an insider's view of these regattas from someone whose seabag always is packed and ready to go, whether it be to Newport; Cowes, England; Long Beach; or the China Sea.

AMERICA'S CUP:
"Do We Go Left, or Right?"

If there is one constant, it is that most of us who sail on the world-class level have been or are now involved with the America's Cup—a venue that puts a premium on ability, experience, and hard work. It is not for the psychologically unsound, the immature, or the problem child. Cup sailors are gifted in some way, as helmsmen, sail trimmers, mastmen; they have to be committed to long months (now years) of mental pressure and physical abrasion, always knowing that the end may take them to the greatest heights or utter disappointment. To have been through it marks you for life.

*   *   *

I didn't know much about the problems ahead when I joined Ted Turner in 1976. The idea of crewing in the America's Cup was the last thing in my mind when I arrived at the Chicago Yacht Club in October of that year to attend a meeting of the U.S. Yacht Racing Union, the body that governs sailboat racing in the United States. I was there to sell the class racing committee on the idea of publishing a junior sailing manual and to get the committee to sponsor sailing seminars. What I found, instead, even before taking off my coat, was that I was being proposed for the Olympic Committee (I had been a member of an ad hoc committee to study American chances in the forthcoming Olympic Games). And then in the cloakroom, here was Ted Turner, already somewhat of a legend, in a sparkling mood. I had not seen him to speak to since we had sailed against each other in a dinghy regatta in Barrington, R.I., four years earlier.

"Jobson," he said as we shook hands, "I remember you. How would you like to be my tactician on *Courageous* next summer?"

The decision came quickly and almost without thinking. I was in one of those periods of lateral movement that people have in their lives. I had been coaching for four years at the U.S. Merchant Marine Academy at Kings Point, N.Y., while Janice and I lived in a cottage in nearby Great Neck. I was ready for a change, and the eight months of commitment to *Courageous* would give me time to think about the future. I had no idea that the involvement with Turner, sailing with him on his own offshore racer, *Tenacious,* and the close alliance with him at that America's Cup would have such a profound effect on my life.

But Turner, I think, knew. Coincidentally, we flew

back to Annapolis together after the USYRU meeting, a flight that seemed to be auspicious; we talked about racing and about tactics and about crew organization, and there was practically nothing we disagreed about, Finally Turner said, "Gary, if you help me, I think you'll also learn a lot about how I conduct business." That cemented it. When we parted, Turner went off to sail in the Annapolis Yacht Club's Fall Series, and I joined the Kings Point sailing team at the U.S. Naval Academy for a regatta. I reflected that I was lucky to be associated with Turner, who, at thirty-seven, not only was becoming a young phenomenon in the business world but who also was without a doubt the most outstanding sailor of the decade.

He had grown up sailing Penguins in the Savannah River during summers, and even at age eight he had picked up the first of the nicknames that would constantly trail him: "Turnover Turner" (from his propensity to capsize). As a teenager he successfully raced Lightnings and then, skipping out of the South to the Ivy League's Brown University in Providence, R.I., won eight major events during his freshman year and continued to win throughout his college career.

Turner, I knew, could sail most boats and win. He had captured the Flying Dutchman and Y-Flyer Nationals. He raced Lightnings successfully, and then broke into ocean racing with his forty-foot *Vamp X,* a boat that took the measure of the Southern Ocean Racing Circuit. Turner showed the fleet that by racing to the maximum every minute you were on the course, you would probably win.

His next major move, I recalled, was buying *American Eagle,* a twelve-meter that had lost her bid as defender in the 1964 and 1967 America's Cup trials. She had been converted to ocean racing, but Turner converted her even further by eliminating her big propeller and dressing her with the newest and best sails he could afford.

With that, *American Eagle* became a legend in her own right, both in the United States and abroad. Turner and *American Eagle* set a Fastnet Race record, won the Sydney–Hobart Race, the Annapolis–Newport Race, and the SORC. The bright red *American Eagle* swept everything. Turner then opted for a smaller racing craft, the thirty-eight-foot one-tonner *Lightnin'*, with which he again won in the Circuit. (The SORC was to be his for many years; not only did he win it several times, but he also placed at the top in sixteen consecutive Circuits, a record that has yet to be broken.)

If there was any personal racing disaster for him, it was in 1974, when he took over the helm of the twelve-meter *Mariner,* a boat that was hopelessly slow and so frustrated him that some of his choice comments came out of that summer ("Even a turd is pointed at both ends"). I had known about that summer's efforts and even briefly considered an offer to join the trials aboard *Valiant,* another twelve that was vying for the defense but obviously didn't have a chance against *Courageous* (newly built in aluminum that year) and the rebuilt *Intrepid.*

But for Turner, rallying is the name of his game, and he came back to defy the disparagers by purchasing the sixty-one-foot racer *Dora IV,* changing her name to *Tenacious,* and embarking on what was to become a new and glorious racing career. That was also going to include *Courageous,* which he had secured as a trial horse for Ted Hood's new twelve-meter *Independence.* By signing on with Turner and *Courageous* I also found myself tactician of *Tenacious* and so at twenty-six began a close seagoing association that lasted for more than four years.

I knew more about Turner, in fact, than I knew about the America's Cup. Despite its ability to capture public attention outside of the yachting ranks, the pursuit of the Cup, with all of the intrigue of yacht selection and crews and the formalities that went along with it, didn't mean much to me. I seemed to be too occupied with racing and coaching to have aspirations for crewing on twelves. During the summer of 1974, after winning the Force Five North Americans (eight straight races against fifty-odd boats), I attended a party at Rosecliff, one of the Newport mansions now owned by the city, just prior to the Cup races between *Courageous* and Australia's *Southern Cross*. Everyone there was from the yachting community, and everyone said, "*Courageous* is going to clean the Aussies' clock" (which it did, four straight). I left the party feeling that if *Courageous* was so superior, racing for the Cup was not such a big deal after all.

What was lost to me at twenty-three, but that I came to understand later, was the aura of the America's Cup. It is a summing up every four years of design research in boats, gear, and sails, a new generation of younger men gradually taking the place of old afterguards and crew—all overlaid by tradition that goes back to 1851, when the schooner *America* went to England and whipped the best of the British racing boats, bringing home the "100 Guineas" Cup—later given to the New York Yacht Club as the America's Cup.

In 1967, for instance, while I was racing as a schoolboy on Barnegat Bay, there still was a connection at the America's Cup in Newport that summer between the pre-World War Two years of competition in the J-boats and the postwar adoption of twelve-meter yachts as proper vehicles to contend for the Cup. Harold S. (Mike) Vanderbilt, a member of the syndicate that sponsored the new defender, *Intrepid,* had beaten back three English challenges in historic J-boat racing in the 1930s. In 1930, at the helm of *Enterprise,* he defeated Sir Thomas Lipton's *Shamrock V.* Four years later he fought off T.O.M. Sopwith's *Endeavour.* After losing the first two races in *Rainbow,* he came from behind to win the third race and then swept the series, winning 4–2. And then, in 1937, in the last of the America's Cup contests in the giant J-class sloops, Vanderbilt, in *Ranger,* handily closed the door on another Sopwith challenge, this time in *Endeavour II.* Vanderbilt then moved on to campaign in a new twelve-meter yacht, *Vim,* in offshore racing. It was designed by the same young genius who had drawn up *Ranger* and a host of other winning yachts in the 1930s, Olin Stephens.

Vim survived the war, as the J-boats didn't (*Ranger* was scrapped for her steel) and became the basis of the New York Yacht Club's decision to switch America's Cup competition to twelve-meter yachts. The much larger J-boats had become too expensive to run, and the NYYC had *Vim* on hand to race. But in 1958, for the first postwar Cup, *Vim* was ridden off the waves by another Stephens design, *Columbia,* which then proceeded to give the British challenger, *Sceptre,* a toasting.

Stephens was another link between the pre- and postwar period in America's Cup racing. A fine sailor as well as an intuitive designer who looked at tank-testing and later computers as means but not ends in yacht architecture, he kept trying to find new ways to make his boats go incrementally faster. *Constellation* succeeded *Columbia* in 1964, and in 1967 *Constellation* was dumped by *Intrepid,* which marked the first radical change in twelve-meter design since the birth of *Vim. Intrepid* was snub-nosed, whereas previous yachts had rounded bows. And she sported a double rudder configuration—a small steering rudder well aft, hung on a bustle and a trimtab relatively far forward on the trailing edge of the keel. The two separate rudders provided less wetted surface and gave *Intrepid* a decided edge over her stablemate, *Constellation,* and her Australian opponent, *Dame Pattie,* which stood no chance against her.

Much of this history I learned later, reading during the nonracing hours in Newport. But the one item I did know was that the boat I was going to sail on had been Stephens's last breakthrough, the first American twelve to be built out of aluminum. Here was a man who had been designing the world's fastest racing boats since 1927; in 1974 two of his designs, *Intrepid* and *Courageous,* slugged it out for the defense, with the popular *Intrepid,* rebuilt by a California syndicate, going bow to bow with the newer boat all summer, until on the very last day gear failure caused her defeat and the selection of *Courageous* by the New York Yacht Club. Now, heading into the fall of 1976, the Stephens connection still was present. *Courageous,* with some clever surgery and restitching by sailmaker/designer Ted Hood, would go as trial horse against a Hood design, *Independence,* in a basically New England effort sponsored by the Kings Point Fund, while a California group headed by sailmaker Lowell North would try to break the eastern grip on defenders with a new Stephens boat, *Enterprise,* and an old Stephens boat, *Intrepid,* as trial horse.

Such comings and goings, and formations and reformations of boats, people, and alliances were familiar stuff in the tight little America's Cup world. But it was not apparent to me, and would not be until I had become deeply involved with it, on my own boat several years later. For now it was simply a matter of following Turner's lead. I had been handed an enormous responsibility, and I wasn't going to let it slide.

In December 1976, *Courageous* and *Independence* sailed against each other off their base at Ted Hood's Little Harbor Boatyard in Marblehead. My first day there, I sailed aboard *Independence,* and watching quietly, it seemed to me that *Courageous* had the boat speed that *Independence* lacked. On the next day I switched to *Courageous* and discovered that there was nothing intimidating about racing a twelve despite the presence of a number of experienced America's Cup hands.

While *Courageous* was supposed to be the trial horse in the stable run by Ted Hood and syndicate manager Lee Loomis, apparently Turner had brought a great deal of Texas money into the syndicate on the very good chance that *Courageous* eventually would go to the line off Newport as the American defender.

John McNamara, a *Sail* magazine contributor, wrote: "As the ice came to Marblehead and the twelves were hauled, the inside line at Matty's Sail Loft, the local spigot of truth, was that *Courageous* and *Independence* were damn even; that *Courageous* had a slight edge to weather in a sea; that *Independence* showed best downwind or all-around in light air. At the Little Harbor Boatyard, there was jauntiness to the *Independence* men. They agreed as to the evenness . . . but pointed with confidence to the changes *Courageous* must undergo to comply with the twelve-meter rule. (In 1974, her hatches were open so that winches could be run from below, a detail that nearly caused the boat to swamp whenever there was a good sea running.) Her decks had to be closed over, her machinery go up on deck, her boom raised, all things that wouldn't help her enough in the end. *Independence* would be the boat of the spring."

With the boats hauled for the winter while alterations were being made, the California syndicate raced *Enterprise* against *Intrepid* and elected Lowell North, a cool perfectionist with a great sense of organization, as skipper. On our side of the United States I sailed with Turner as tactician aboard *Tenacious* in the Southern Ocean Racing Circuit, and we took a second in Class A. Then we went cross-country to the Congressional Cup in Long Beach, Calif., where we came in first, defeating both Ted Hood and Lowell North. The Southern Ocean Racing Circuit and the Congressional Cup were my first two regattas with Turner, and we were off to a successful start. We seemed to work well together at sea; his sailing style was similar to mine in that he liked to tack the boat slowly, was aggressive with his sail changes, and really understood how to work with the sails to keep a boat moving. He was accurate at the helm and had a great sense of tactics, which I was expected to reinforce by giving him input. He forced decisions. "Tell me right now," he would say sharply as we picked up a wind shift, "do we go left or right?"

In the spring, we began spending weekends in Marblehead, speed-testing with *Independence,* pressing her in the still-icy waters off the North Shore. There would be no formal racing until Newport, but still it seemed to me that *Courageous* was the faster boat.

Turner had entrusted me with organizing the crew, an intensive job that kept me out of the political line of fire. There was a lot going on beyond the docks that was not the crew's to think about; 1977 became the first year in which commercial considerations were part of the America's Cup scene. Much of the battle was over sails, specifically which sails were going to be used on *Courageous*—Hood or North.

In 1974, the Hood monopoly on twelve-meter sails had been shattered when *Intrepid,* a California boat, went with North, and *Courageous* was rigged with sails from both lofts. Now, in 1977, it mattered very much to the future marketing success of Ted Hood and Lowell North, both helmsmen of their own boats, whose sails would be pictured when the press came to Newport for the trials and Cup finals. Caught in the middle was Ted Turner, a self-proclaimed amateur, who wanted North as well as Hood headsails for *Courageous* and prevailed upon the syndicate to let him have them.

North, however, refused, on the grounds that he had an exclusive contract with the *Enterprise* syndicate. And Turner, by now in Newport, turned on North in a confrontation that featured the bitter Turner at his vitriolic worst. It was the angriest I had ever seen Turner as he raged at the quiet, relatively mild-mannered North to the point where the California sailmaker was in tears.

But Turner had made his psychological point. To the world he said, "Hell, I'm the only amateur in the deal. The pros won't sell me any sails." With that, as the June trials started in Newport, Turner had found his way into the hearts and minds of his countrymen, an image, as John McNamara wrote: "There comes Robert E. (Ted) Turner. The key to his selection will be his inner conviction he is riding a winner from the outset. Turner can rise to the Southern élan of a George Pickett leading his gray legions through the wheatfields into a maw of Union artillery on Gettysburg's Cemetery Ridge."

Turner already had the media watching him. In his first year as owner of the Atlanta Braves, he had managed to get on the wrong side of baseball commissioner Bowie Kuhn and find himself banned for a year for player tampering. In the eyes of the yachting establishment, where things were done "in a certain way," many seasoned Cup followers were not routing for *Courageous*. The respectable Hood and North, known quantities in their speech (laconic) and conduct (exemplary), would fight it out for the defense. Mr. Turner and his boat would be "excused" by the Selection Committee and return to his native turf.

What they didn't understand, and those of us aboard *Courageous* did understand (especially the *Tenacious* crew members) was that Turner was a very good sailor and really wanted to win. He knew he had a very fast boat, and the anger of being refused North sails stayed with him. We went into the June trials off Newport with very little fanfare; as far as the America's Cup summer was concerned, Newport still was asleep.

But it didn't take the local citizenry long to wake up and start opening new bank accounts for the money that would flow in. *Courageous* won nine of ten races in the June trials, and the media began focusing on Turner.

"Terrible Ted Takes Command" was the cover story in *Sports Illustrated*'s July 4 issue. Coles Phinizy wrote,

In Turner there is some of the ambidextrous genius of da Vinci as well as the quick wits of an alley cat. Tilting against the very best in a second-hand boat—if indeed *Courageous* may be called

that—is an experience Turner can relish. . . .
Winning big is not his style. He thrives on squeak-
ers. He loves to battle with his back against the
wall. If there is no wall close by he will go miles
out of his way to find one. After he beat Hood
convincingly by about a minute in two shortened
races . . . he was somewhat moody. When he beat
North by 45 seconds in one race, then poked two
feet of his bow across the finish line to take another, he was more cheerful. On another day, after
he slowly ate away a one-minute 35-second deficit
through five legs and lost to North by seven seconds, and then in the second matchup changed leads
with North twice to win by 22 seconds, he was
jubilant.

In July the pattern changed, and suddenly as the trials
got under way again, we slowed down. It wasn't tactics and it wasn't crew work. It was boat speed; we
were off the pace. Turner and I had long discussions as
we walked to the boat from Conley Hall, the monastic
mansion that was our headquarters and residence hall.
We talked about tactics and what we might or might
not be doing wrong and we talked about Turner's goals
and we talked about world and business affairs. The
morning walks had the effect of calming the ever-ner-
vous skipper, but they had little effect on boat speed;
by the end of the month we had a losing streak, and
going back over every race it became apparent what
was happening. Our sails, at the leading edge of Hood
Dacron technology, had been used up in June. Blown
out and tired, they were simply incapable of keeping
Courageous competitive.
Turner set about getting the syndicate to come up

with new sails for the most important tests of the summer, the August final trials from which the defending yacht would be chosen. Despite the handicap under which *Courageous* labored, July was an important month for me because along with deciding whether to go "left" or "right" I seem to have accepted the responsibility of keeping Turner cool. In reality, what little I knew about match racing I was learning from him. But I did what he needed most: fed him information about our progress relative to the other boat, called wind shifts, and tried to be calm outwardly, which wasn't the way I felt on the inside.

A perceptive reporter, however, had been watching the two of us. "Patience of Jobson May Be the Key to Turner's Success at Cup Trials," *The New York Times* headlined at the end of July. Bill Wallace wrote, "Gary Jobson . . . has the stickiest job of all among the 77 sailors competing . . . here this summer. Jobson's title is tactician aboard *Courageous,* but there is more to it than that. He also serves as guru, as shrink, as confidant and nursemaid for Ted Turner, the volatile skipper of *Courageous* whose moods range from infectious enthusiasm to infectious gloom."

"I try to do what I'm told and shut up," Turner told Wallace. "And I find that awfully difficult."

For my part, Wallace quoted me as saying, "I try to talk with an even tone in my voice and always stress the positive. I don't want him to get excited or depressed. If we can keep him quiet and concentrating, the boat really goes and no one can beat us.

"We agree about ninety percent of the time. He'll fight me some of the time, but we work it out. I'm blessed with awfully good eyes. I think I can see the wind shifts and call them before they reach us and that helps."

What also helped is that Robby Doyle, our master sailmaker and trimmer who worked for Hood Sails, was able to get a new main and a new jib cut in time for the last race of the July series with the blessing of the syndicate. Like a football team that has been trailing but scores a touchdown in the last two minutes of the first half to go into the locker room ahead, *Courageous* won the last race against *Enterprise*. With all of Lowell North's new sail technology on his side, including his first experiments with Kevlar cloth—a new fabric that later revolutionized the sail industry (Kevlar is stronger but lighter than Dacron), Turner used *Courageous'* new beautifully cut Dacron sails to pilot the boat to a come-from-behind victory over *Enterprise*. This was Turner meat; come-from-behind victories are what he is all about.

That night he said, very quietly but confidently, "We are going to go all the way, Gary." He had decided that we were going to win, and there would be no stopping *Courageous*. Then, in a move that would be unheard of in the pressure cooker of today's America's Cup competition, he gave the crew a psychological boost by allowing everyone to take a few days off before the August trials began. In the two weeks between trials we sailed only ten days. But Turner was looking forward to reentering the competition. "I'm going to enjoy the August trials," he said.

The result was that we went into the final trials with new sails and a confident crew buoyed by the optimistic Turner, who had welded a team that trusted each other, accepted criticism, and worked very well together. Like a revivalist exhorting his flock, Turner was inspirational. "Jobson," he would say, "you are going to be a household name when this is over. You can do it." One day he said to Robby Doyle, "You are going to be the best sailmaker and everyone is going to know it."

Turner forced everyone to find the key to themselves. "Do well in sailing," he told us, "and you'll do well in that larger world out there."

Doing well in sailing, for Turner, meant hewing to discipline. The rules were simple: Be on time and sail hard. *Courageous* left the dock at 9:30 A.M., without fail. If you weren't there, the boat would sail without you. The rule was invoked to make sure that all repairs were done in time; there was no "just ten minutes more and she'll be ready."

As the August races got under way, all crew meetings were held on the boat as we went out to combat *Independence* and *Enterprise* or whoever was in the lists for the day. There was no general conversation, especially with Turner, who wanted nothing but constant input. General conversation was left for our early-morning walks through the back streets and public ways of Newport and evenings, while we sat in his room and watched baseball (Turner had installed a satellite dish at Conley Hall so he could follow the fortunes of his estranged Atlanta Braves).

Courageous picked up steam and was unbeatable. By the end of the selection period we were 10–1, losing one race when a running backstay broke. The stream of victories made it easy for the New York Yacht Club selection committee. The other two boats had been excused, and when the gentlemen in their blazers and gray fedoras arrived to announce their choice, Turner forgot himself momentarily and hugged committee chairman George Hinman, a very proper sort of person who had been involved with the 1974 Cup and had seen Turner humiliated while sailing on *Mariner,* the hopelessly slow twelve-meter that had tried to beat *Courageous*.

So it was to be *Courageous* against Alan Bond's *Australia,* which had defeated French and Swedish yachts in the foreign eliminations. Turner again took the pressure off between the end of the trials and the beginning of the Cup races by leaving Newport and getting us into the Vineyard Race, a four-day furlough that cleared our minds and got us ready for the Cup.

For me, it was one of the best times of my life. I had done the job set before me by Turner a year earlier. We had succeeded in defeating two new American yachts, and getting the call from the New York Yacht Club to defend the historic trophy against yet another Australian challenge from the tireless Alan Bond. I had accepted a job as the head varsity sailing coach at the U.S. Naval Academy. In Newport, in the golden afternoons of fall, with smoky sou'westers blowing out of Block Island Sound, we came back from practice to see the town's clock steeple and the Hill section around it lit by the late sunshine, and all was right with the world.

Turner was saying, as if to prove it to himself, "Well, it ain't such a big deal," but the crew, knowing him better than he did himself, asked me to take him on an extra-long walk on the first day of the Cup so they could get the boat prepared without him being around. It was to no avail; Turner arrived at the boat before the crew did.

We left the dock that first morning amid great fanfare and cheering and blowing of horns and sirens, but not many boats seemed to be accompanying us, and Turner said again, "See, it's not that big a deal." But an hour later, as we approached the America's Cup buoy, we could see an armada waiting for us—Coast

Guard cutters and picket boats, big yachts owned by the syndicate supporters, sightseeing vessels as well as small sailboats, the Goodyear blimp, and what appeared to be squadrons of helicopters and private aircraft. It *was* a big deal; like the football playoffs, the trials didn't matter. This was the Super Bowl. This was what mattered.

"In what has to be one of the most dramatic moments in sports," Jeff Spranger wrote in *Sail,* "the first windward leg of the first Cup race becomes the acid test of the mettle of the challenge. If ever a challenger is going to win the America's Cup, she will have to prove in that first decisive leg that she has the edge in speed and that her crew knows tactically how to take advantage of that edge."

We decided on a port tack start at the committee boat. *Australia* went off on starboard and then covered and for the first fifteen minutes, like boxers feeling each other out, both boats went for speed. *Courageous* fatefully drew ahead and tacked across *Australia*'s bow. Then *Australia* tacked away and we tacked to cover and I looked over at Turner for the first time, having been concentrating on my own job. He was perspiring under his engineer's cap as he steered intently. In a normal tone I said, "Well, they ain't slow." Turner replied, "Yeah, but they ain't fast, either," implying that *Courageous* couldn't be stopped.

The margin at the windward mark was twelve boat lengths, and from that point on we were never behind at any mark over the next three races as *Australia* went down to defeat, 4–0. For most of us on the crew the races went by in a blur, with decreasing pressure the more we won. One evening, while being towed back to Newport, Turner looked at the huge fleet escorting us home and said, "We have to enjoy these days because whatever we do in the rest of our lives, the times will never be as good as these are."

On the frenzied night after the last race, there were bottles of Dom Perignon handed aboard, and it seemed as if everyone in Newport and possibly the world cared about *Courageous*. In retrospect it was the colorful Turner the world was behind; he drew increasing attention to himself and the America's Cup. From June through September the press corps grew dramatically. They cheered as he walked into the news conference at the National Guard armory, and when it seemed that he obviously had celebrated too much (Turner was not a drinker) and fell off his chair, that was all right, too.

The next day, he was sheepish about it, but it didn't matter because it was all over. Like the Super Bowl, everyone had filed out of the stands and gone home. Turner returned to Atlanta, and I went to Annapolis to begin a new phase of my life.

COWES WEEK—FASTNET RACE: "We Like It This Way. . . ."

It was blowing twenty-five knots as our ferry approached the Isle of Wight. The fleet of fifty-seven Admiral's Cup yachts sporting supergraphics rivaling anything at Indianapolis Raceway surfed by on wild spinnaker runs. But the Red Funnel ferry, on its own mission, paid them no attention and just bulled through the fleet, scattering the vessels like a fox in a henhouse.

Cowes Week is made up of a series of races that includes events for over forty different classes. The boats range from fifteen-foot dinghies all the way up to maxiyachts. In fact, in 1985, the old J-boat *Valsheda* also took part in the activities.

In 1957, to increase international competition, the combined yacht clubs of Cowes on the Isle of Wight decided to host the Admiral's Cup competition. Every other year representatives from as many as twenty countries send three boats each as part of a team. The Americans have won this event only twice, in 1969 and 1971. In the odd-number years the final event of Cowes Week is the grueling Fastnet race. Cowes Week may be the single largest sailing event in the world.

It was August 1979 and I was heading for Cowes for the first time to participate in a week of racing with Ted Turner aboard *Tenacious* in the place where yacht racing had been born 150 years earlier. Since that week, which was to end up in glory as well as uncommon disaster in the Fastnet Race, I have been at Cowes two more times. Each time I have marveled at the uncompromising style of the British in stubbornly refusing to change an event in which trouble always is lurking around the corner. The British are tough that way; Racing at Cowes, which dates back to 1829, is as much part of the social season as Ascot or Wimbledon, and is under the sponsorship of the Royal Yacht Squadron. The royal yacht *Britannia* is always anchored within public view and is escorted by a pair of Royal Navy frigates. And Prince Philip and other royal young persons may well be in the racing fleet somewhere. In fact, in the 1979 Britannia Cup, the premier day race during Cowes Week, Prince Charles was a member of the afterguard of the seventy-seven-foot sloop *Siska,* which crossed the line first ahead of 107 other entrants and placed third on corrected time (*Tenacious* won the Cup).

What gives Cowes its very special flavor besides the royal presence is the hazards with which the venue abounds. Like a golf course on some windy headland in Scotland, the Solent, on which much of the racing is done, is full of traps for the unwary. It's a mean piece of water about five miles across from the southern coast of England and about twenty miles long. The Solent's leading characteristic is its ten-foot tides. The place is full of shoals, which appear suddenly when the tide runs out. In fact, the late designer Uffa Fox, one of Britain's yachting heroes who lived in Cowes, invented a form of golf that was played at low tide; the participants sailed from one "green" (shoal) to another. Currents race in the Solent constantly at about three to four knots, and boats continually run aground on the beaches.

As if this isn't all yachtsmen have to contend with, there also are hazards manufactured by man to test the mettle of any sailor who may think he or she has seen it all. All races start off the Royal Yacht Squadron on the Cowes waterfront, using an imaginary transit for a starting line about a mile long; the line always is the same, without regard to wind direction. The armada of eight hundred racing boats maneuvers in the vicinity of the starting line, crossing tacks with ferries, hydrofoils, hovercraft, and spectator boats. It could be raining, it could be foggy, it could be blowing twenty knots of wind or no wind at all. Collisions are common. In 1979, at the start of the Channel Race, seven yachts were forced to drop out because of collisions, which prompted the commodore of the Royal Yacht Squadron to say at the awards ceremony, "I know many people have complained about the way we race here and, in fact, sailing is very tough but we like it that way and invite those who want to live up to the competition."

Naturally, with eight hundred or more boats in the area, the competition is going to extend landward after the day's last guns. Yachts raft along the Cowes River in tiers of ten. Restaurants and watering holes overflow at all hours. The royal family entertains and is entertained at black-tie affairs. The crews hit the pubs, and sometimes fireworks ensue. In 1979, things went wild. Among other things, a beer tent was burned down and a crew woke up one morning to find the hull of their boat completely covered with feathers, this deemed fitting punishment for participating in too many collisions.

On Saturday of that August week of 1979, it was almost a pleasure to get away from it all as we took the starting gun on the flood tide and headed out for Fastnet Rock. Sponsored by the Royal Ocean Racing Club, the sixty-one-year-old Fastnet Race is one of the premier ocean races, a 605-mile affair that ranks in length with the Newport–Bermuda, Sydney–Hobart, and China Sea races. The Fastnet, even in good weather, isn't particularly pleasant, because it takes the yachts west along the southern coast of England, where they have to deal with heavy currents and some noted headlands with their attendant dangers, the Needles, Portland Bill, the Eddystone rocks, and the Lizard. It continues northwest across the Irish Sea to the notorious Fastnet Rock, an ugly piece of crag with a lighthouse that serves as a turning mark. On the way back, the fleet passes south of the Scillies and Bishop's Rock, then heads up the English Channel, past the same headlands to the finish line in Plymouth.

We didn't have any problems getting out of the Solent, but no one had told us about the overfalls and tidal rip off Portland Bill. Fighting the tide, we tried to break through, and I called for a tack in order not to be swept away by the current. But the maneuver was useless; for three hours we sat in the grip of the overfalls until the tide changed.

By this time a pea-soup fog had descended as *Tenacious,* under the sagacious eye of navigator Peter Bowker, worked its way along the southern coast. *Tenacious* had a light reacher on board that was really fast and the Hood loft had made another fast sail for the boat called a flanker, a kind of flat spinnaker. Between the light reacher and the flanker, *Tenacious* left the fleet, passed Land's End to starboard in the fog, and headed under spinnaker across the Irish Sea to Fastnet Rock.

Turner had said very little up to this point, although he had gathered the crew on deck before the start to tell us, "There are three hundred and five boats in this race. I want to win it more than anything else in my career." Now Bowker, as unruffled as ever, had come on deck to tell Turner that the weather bureau was forecasting a severe Force 9 to 11 storm for the area. Turner's first reaction was to go below and check his copy of Bowditch (*The American Practical Navigator*) for the precise meaning of Force 11 (fifty-six to sixty-three knots, violent storm, heavy waves). He said, "My God, Force Eleven we're going to have?" Then he began getting everyone prepared for the storm.

We rigged jackstays (to clip harnesses to) and put on dry clothes and foul-weather gear. He had the cook prepare a hot meal for all hands. Everyone was rested, fed, and felt strong and prepared. When the storm hit, we had already rounded Fastnet and were heading back down the Irish Sea. By midnight, with the wind blowing a steady forty knots and beginning to gust higher, Turner relieved me at the helm, saying, "Okay, Jobson, you're off now for four hours. I want you out of those wet clothes and get your dry clothes on because I need you." Turner stayed at the helm until 4:00 A.M., guiding the boat flawlessly, then went below, forcing himself to rest. By this time *Tenacious* had been stripped of her mainsail in an all-hands operation and was sailing on her No. 4 storm jib only. At the wheel it was almost impossible to see because of the driving spray, and with only the small jib up, steering was difficult—searching for a middle way between sailing too low and having to tack away from the Scilly Isles, and luffing and destroying the sail. Despite everything, we kept the boat moving, picking out by their lights other boats in the race, some drifting, others trying to keep control without sails.

"Look out, red light ahead, now green!" one of the crew would yell above the storm, and I would try to work around the approaching lights on the boats sailing in the opposite direction. By this time radio reports were coming in suggesting the dimensions of the disaster. Helicopters crisscrossed in the violent winds, searching for abandoned boats and life rafts.

But only Bowker and Turner knew the full story. Apparently Turner had decided that if the crew worked together, the strongly constructed boat could be kept going, and feeding radio reports of the disaster would only cripple morale. At dawn the scope of the waves (some said sixty feet) could be seen and felt. They were monstrous and steep; it was a tribute to *Tenacious* that she held together with little damage and a tribute to

Turner that he knew his boat and his crew so well that he could bring them to victory. It was only after we docked at Plymouth that we understood what we had been through and the extent of the disaster created by the storm—fifteen dead; twenty-four boats abandoned; and 136 persons saved by helicopter crews, the Navy, or commercial or private vessels. It was a race never to be forgotten by those who participated in it, and it spurred great changes in the rules for participation and for the gear to be carried on board. We had won through perseverance, experience, good seamanship, Turner's leadership, and *Tenacious*' heart, which never gave out. To this day Ted Turner considers this his greatest victory.

I returned to Cowes twice more for the week's festivities and racing and especially to sail in the Fastnet. In 1981 I joined Dennis Conner aboard the newly launched eighty-one-foot maxiboat *Condor* as tactician and in the doing, learned as much about Conner, who had won the America's Cup the previous year in *Freedom*, as I did about racing maxiboats.

The racing during the week, especially between the maxis, the new *Condor* and her sister ship *Kialoa* (also eighty-one feet), was inconclusive because of the light air—a great contrast with Cowes Week two years earlier, when the wind never seemed to drop below twenty knots.

Fastnet was no exception. It was a light-air start, with both *Condor* and *Kialoa* going over the line early. We were the last class to start and because of the penalty found ourselves dead last in the race, boat for boat.

Conner, I discovered, has a nice tactical sense and a good eye for the wind shifts. As we worked our way along the coast, Connor noticed a shift about four miles along the shoreline where the wind was going to bend to the right, about fifty degrees. We headed over in that direction, looking odd doing it, but caught the shift and surged into the lead over *Kialoa*.

Conner has his own unique feel for handling an opponent. For instance, in a race, if you come up and tack on him, he won't tack away immediately, but coast up to where your breeze is and then tack, forcing you into a double tack. It's a nice tactic, one of many the clever Conner has up his sleeve.

Kialoa moved into a small lead after passing Fastnet and Conner seemed calm, very relaxed, and patient. The two maxis had moved ahead so that the rest of the fleet was at least a hundred miles behind us. But the wind was disappearing. I went off watch thinking that in fifteen hours or so we would be at the finish line. When I woke up, racing to get my gear on to come on deck, I realized there was no motion; *Condor* had dropped her anchor to keep from being swept back by the tide. Here we were in an area of the sea where the waves had been as high as forty-five feet two years earlier, and now we were anchored in a flat calm, waiting for the tide to change.

Kialoa was in the same fix about a mile away and so were some 270 other boats, just waiting for a breeze that finally filled in and blew *Kialoa* to the finish line twenty minutes ahead of *Condor*. When *Condor* finally arrived in Plymouth in the darkness, flares lit up the sky, revealing hundreds of people along the shore waiting to see the boats. But all I wanted to do was disappear into the train station and head home.

In 1985, I came back to Cowes with the fifty-four-foot German Frers-designed *Jubilation,* a boat I had

helped create (see Chapter V). There were three nota-
ble happenings: a near-collision with Prince Philip, a
near-wipeout with Prince Michael of Kent aboard, and
a Fastnet Race that had all of the makings of another
1979 destruction derby but never got stormy enough
to parallel the earlier event.

At the 1985 Cowes Week, British royalty took the
yachting events as seriously as they had done since the
days before World War I when the King of England
and Germany's Kaiser watched their respective yachts
race each other. (The British always won.) On this oc-
casion, Prince Philip, a good sailor who had raced for
many years with British author and designer Uffa Fox,
found himself in a contretemps with *Jubilation*. In the
lead after rounding a mark in one of the races with
what appeared to be several hundred boats behind us,
we crossed ahead of several vessels that hadn't turned
yet, including a Yeoman XXIII with Prince Philip at
the helm. *Jubilation* was to leeward of him and hence
had right of way. Intently concentrating on his steering, he didn't see us until the last second. With quick
response he went head to wind with the spinnaker in a
mess, and the boat became stuck in irons. With some
embarrassment he peered at us from under his natty
white hat as we swept by.

In another race aboard *Jubilation*, British yachting
journalist Bob Fisher, a friend of the great and near-
great, had invited Prince Michael of Kent aboard on a
particularly nasty day with the wind blowing about
thirty knots true. Going downwind under spinnaker,
the boat seemed on the verge of going out of control
as we continually surfed, sailing by the lee to try to
make the leeward mark.

Prince Michael stood far aft along with the American

owner, Jack James, both holding on tightly to keep from being swept off. At the helm, trying to keep the boat from broaching as the spinnaker oscillated because of the heavy breeze, I said, "I'm going to lose it here. Maybe we should take the spinnaker down. Or does someone feel they could do a better job steering?" Fisher, an experienced sailor and never one to resist a challenge, said he could do it and took the wheel.

After a few hundred yards at breakneck speed, Fisher lost control and the boat did a full wipeout. We put the spinnaker pole about ten feet into the water with the mast lying parallel to the horizon and the rudder lifted out of the sea. The spinnaker, loaded with water, held the boat down on her side. The cockpit filled, too, not only with water but also with Fisher and the owner, a rotund, 260-pound person, on top of the prince. All were soaking wet.

Finally the spinnaker tore apart, releasing the boat, and we got everything under control and rounded the mark. Prince Michael hadn't said a word until, as we headed up upwind, he leaned over to me at the wheel. "Gary," he asked quietly, "I wonder if, ah, you could explain to me precisely what happened?"

The Fastnet made the news that year, not only in England but also worldwide because of the strange mishap that befell the British Whitbread Round-the-World Race entry, *Drum*. The vessel lost its keel and capsized, trapping for a short time its owner, British rock star Simon Le Bon, and five of the crew in the cabin. The others had scrambled to safety on the overturned hull. Fortunately the accident occurred close enough to shore to get a Navy helicopter very quickly to the rescue. And also fortunately, an experienced Navy frogman had the coolness to lead the trapped crew out from inside the cabin.

On *Jubilation*, we knew nothing of that as we tried to deal with our own problems. With the wind blowing thirty knots at the start, our brand-new mainsail refused to stay in the luff groove on the mast and we were forced to take down the mainsail and beat out of the Solent under a small No. 4 headsail during a very uncomfortable night. Luckily we had an old mainsail as a spare. It was slow, but better than no mainsail at all.

In the morning, the wind continued to build until we were forced to sail under a Dacron No. 5 jib (about as small as you can get) and a storm trysail substituting for the main. We had 450 square feet of sail up, about the equivalent of a pocket handkerchief for a boat in *Jubilation*'s class, and yet the speedometer was ticking off 7.8 knots, hard on the wind.

We spent eight hours under reduced sail, totally soaked from having had an all-hands call to take down the main. The wind continued at a steady forty knots but it didn't appear, based on weather reports fed to us by the navigator, again Peter Bowker, that we were facing anything like the 1979 storm. But I had learned my lesson well from Turner's example, shortening sail in advance of the bad weather and making sure that the crew had a hot meal early and that they rested while off watch. I also stuck to my regular watches—not tiring myself out by steering continuously, but resting four hours off watch and handing the helm to others in the crew so I would be alert in case of emergencies.

Fortunately there was no emergency for us, but 150 other yachts, fearing a repeat of the 1979 race, had bowed out. There were fourteen dismastings and the accident on *Drum* to complete the picture. Aboard *Jubilation,* crew morale was high, knowing they and the boat had been able to take it.

Once we reached Fastnet Rock, the weather featured squall after squall interspersed with a continuing drizzle in winds ranging from twenty to thirty-five knots. The end of the race became an almost continuous reach as the remaining boats went for speed.

It turned out to be one of the fastest Fastnets ever. The American maxi *Nirvana* shattered the race record by finishing thirteen hours faster than the course had ever been covered before. *Nirvana* traveled 605 nautical miles in just sixty hours for an amazing ten-knot average. *Jubilation* didn't do so badly either: We placed seventh, covering the course in seventy-three hours, fifty-one minutes, with an average speed of 8.2 knots.

Fastnet remains one of the most fascinating races in the world—a true test of seamanship, navigation, and seaworthiness of both ship and sailor. The currents are fickle, the weather is unorthodox. With the royal Ocean Racing Club learning the lessons of 1979 well and instituting new safeguards, including boat-size and experience qualifications, there is no reason that Fastnet shouldn't continue for another sixty years. But no one should forget to bring polypropaline long johns. This is latitude fifty-two degrees north, and it gets pretty cold out there.

MATCH RACING AROUND THE WORLD:
Hauled into the Panel Beaters

The most exciting development in international competition has been the growth of a match-race circuit. In recent years I have had the opportunity to sail in all the major events in places such as Auckland, New Zealand, in the Citizens Cup Match Race series; the Lymington Cup in Lymington, England; the Congressional Cup in Long Beach; the Liberty Cup in New York City; the Great Cities Challenge in Annapolis; and the PBS Australia Cup in Perth, Australia. In addition, there are events in Antibes, France, and Bermuda that I have not participated in.

Match racing is completely different from normal sailboat racing because you race against only one other boat at a time. In this game there really is no second. It is like a wrestling match: One man walks off the mat a winner and the other a loser.

Several of these events are commercially sponsored. For example, the Liberty Cup in New York City, the Australia Cup, and the New Zealand regatta will pay for tickets for competitors to fly in from around the world. Originally the match-race circuit was used for local clubs to bring in top-name sailors; by crewing for these legends and racing against them, local organizers hoped the knowledge would rub off, and it did.

But as has been the trend in all of world-class sailing, the match-race circuit has become more competitive. In the 1986 Liberty Cup, for example, each of the eight crews from the eight competing nations carried passports of the country they represented. Some of the crews—for example, from New Zealand, Australia, Japan, and Italy—arrived with coaches.

The match-race world circuit has become my favorite type of sailing because skippers must adapt their skills to boats they generally have not sailed before, but all are evenly matched. In fact, the race organizers go to great lengths to equalize the boats by standardizing the tension on the rigging, providing computer-cut sails and weighing the boats. The name of the game here is a test of tactical skill and boat-handling technique and not a contest of the yacht designer. Manufacturers have found that providing boats for these events has been a good way to generate sales and interest in their product.

Credit the Long Beach Yacht Club, sponsors of the Congressional Cup, for having started the whole thing twenty-two years ago. It was an idea that caught the imagination of America's foremost sailors—invite the best skippers (and crews) to the boats, and race in larger one-design vessels so there is not only a premium on good tactics but crew work as well. The Congressional Cup, as a result, has been a total success. Long Beach, in March, is the place to be; every top sailor in the country, Olympic veterans and prospects, America's Cup skippers and personnel and ranking foreign invitees are on the course. Onlookers (hundreds take to the water to watch the nine races that comprise the regatta) can see assembled in one place the likes of Lowell North, Ted Turner, Dick Deaver, Dennis Conner, England's Harold Cudmore, and Italy's Mauro Pellaschier. The races are held in Catalina 38s supplied by owners and manufacturers. As of 1985, crews change boats every night.

The success of the Congressional Cup spawned others. Second to get started was the Lymington Cup, sponsored by the Royal Lymington Yacht Club. Lymington, on the edge of the Solent, is one of the yachting centers of England, a place so crowded with boats that if they are not in marinas they are moored on poles tied fore and aft in the water. Typical of the Solent, the current is unpredictable but strong, the tides are high, and the weather predictable—usually nasty. On my last

visit to the Lymington Cup, the boats—Westerly 32s—
all sailed with double-reefed mains and No. 4 storm
jibs. "'Bit of a breeze, what?" said our hosts at the Royal
Lymington. It was blowing twenty-five to thirty knots.
But that didn't faze Princess Anne of England, who
was out in a small rubber dinghy watching the races.
At Lymington, the scheme for running the event is
somewhat different than on other world courses; a round
robin eliminates entrants until there is a final four who
have a sailoff for the Cup.

After you have done at least one circumnavigation
of the world match-race circuit, you discover the dif-
ferences among the regattas, and it is the changes of
scene and the local racing customs that make them fun.
Each has its own personality, depending, for instance,
on whether you rotate boats and how you rotate them.
The rule book is as intensely studied the night before
the first race as a college history text before a final exam.
Starting lines are all set differently. Some have five-
minute starts and some have ten-minute starts. And the
courses vary from regatta to regatta. Some are trian-
gular. Some are windward–leeward. At a few of the
regattas the racers go twice around the course; at others, only once. Some start and finish at the bottom of
the course, some in the middle. At one or two of the
regattas, all the sailors are international; at others, the
crews are local and the skippers are international.

The environment also changes from place to place.
At Perth, the contest for the Australia Cup is held in
Viking 30s (a fourteen-year-old Ben Lexcen design) in
the Swan River, a narrow waterway made even more
narrow by the two hundred boats that come out to
watch. The Aussies televise the regatta and use videocameras to train their own crews for the two weeks

prior to the races. This puts foreigners at a disadvantage: In the last Australia Cup the locals placed first and third.

In New Zealand, where sailboat racing is taken seriously enough to warrant national television coverage, the Citizens Cup races are held in the antipodean autumn near Auckland's North Head, at the edge of the open ocean. Big squalls constantly sweep over the course while the boats, very fast local sloops called Stewart 34s, race within the view of TV cameras and large crowds on North Head.

Each of the thirty-year-old sloops has a name beginning with "P." In one Citizens Cup regatta I skippered *Pioneer* with a typical top-flight New Zealand or Kiwi crew. They were all seasoned competitors. One had just completed the Whitbread Round and the World Race, one had just placed sixth in the 470 World Championships, and another had won the New Zealand Olympic trials in Solings. One of the crew had taken a fourth in the Finn Olympic trials, and two were regulars aboard the Stewarts.

We were allowed two days to practice and familiarize ourselves with each other's strong and weak points and mesh as a crew. We were going against ten of the best skippers in the world, practically all of whom were involved with America's Cup and big-boat racing. By the end of the week we had raced nine times, one against the other, to produce the ultimate winner, Terry McLaughlin, the skipper of the Canadian America's Cup challenger, *Canada I*.

It was tough, give-no-quarter racing of the type that suits the Kiwis and suited me as well. On one very tight maneuver, my tactician said, "Be careful or we'll be hauled into the panel beaters." Intent on steering, I mumbled something unintelligible. "Panel beaters, mate,'" he said, "'what you call an auto body shop." We placed third in 1985.

It was a far different story in the 1981 Congressional Cup. I had sailed as crew in three previous events, but this was to be the first as skipper. It is always an honor to be invited to the Congressional Cup, knowing you will be racing among the very best. But this regatta took an unusual twist for our team aboard a Catalina 38 that hated going downwind. The crew included veteran tactician Andy Rose as well as Conn Findlay, John Wright, Duby Joslin, Tom Relyea, and Kim Roberts— all good men and true whose collective twelve-meter racing experience included berths on *Freedom* and *Courageous* (all three times), *Valiant, Mariner, Clipper, Australia, Gretel II, Southern Cross, Heritage, Intrepid,* and *Enterprise.* With an America's Cup crowd like that, how could things go wrong?

The winner of the Congressional Cup traditionally wins the Crimson Blazer, a prize that had been given to the ten skippers who had won the event in the sixteen times it had been run up to that year. The last-place finisher is awarded a copy of Arthur Knapp's classic volume *Race Your Boat Right.* For us it became a battle for the book and not for the blazer.

Actually, we had great hopes for our boat. In fact, in nine races, we were first at the windward mark six times, beating Rod Davis, who eventually won the regatta, and beating Dick Deaver, a two-time winner, and four of the other competitors. According to the brochure published by the Long Beach Yacht Club, the yacht that reaches the windward mark first after winning the start usually goes on to win. We were to rewrite history.

The downwind leg was our undoing. Establishing comfortable four- to five-boat-length leads going to windward had made us so complacent that our favorite form of spinnaker flying seemed to be in the shape of an hourglass.

"We're gonna get the book if it happens again," I exhorted my crew. Encouraged by my remarks, the spinnaker went up right, but even so, boats would slowly float by us on the short downwind legs.

There were some rays of hope. On the second windward leg of this twice-around windward–leeward course, we would make up time. But when we reached the windward mark, the other boat would zoom away from us downwind. It was not always the result of spinnaker work but boat speed. Our craft simply was unhappy about proceeding downwind.

At the Congressional Cup you race each other competitor once, and you continue on. Therefore, we kept going. But race after race was the same—great start, good windward leg, and then the other boat goes by downwind.

Now, in the last few races, we were ready for the showdown. Would the book be ours? One of the contests was with a U.S. Naval Academy Sailing Squadron crew led by Scott Perry; they were not doing particularly well, either.

We clearly waxed Perry and his team at the start and held on to an advantage on the windward leg. But playing the wind better with greater speed, they blanketed us downwind and went by for the leeward mark. On the second windward leg the lead changed twice in the varying thirty-degree wind shifts, but once again the Academy team came out on top.

It looked hopeless now on the second leeward leg,

but the wind died, and taking advantage of a new breeze for the first time, our boat actually began to move downwind. We rounded the last mark within a length of our foes and even felt we would have an edge on this last weather leg; but alas, the wind shifted once, it was a fifty-fifty coin toss on which tack to take, and we called it wrong. The Perry group went sliding by and we lost our biggest lead of the regatta. The book was almost on my shelf with three races to go.

In the next one, we came up against Dennis Conner. The lead changed five times in the race and by some miracle we ended up lumbering through his lee on the last windward leg. Conner's boat, it seemed, was as cranky as ours; it had blazing speed downwind and nothing to weather.

The next two races were again the same: good start, good windward leg, let the competition roll by downwind again. Included in the disaster was one leeward mark that saw us rounding up and tacking with our chute up, our jib down, and our spinnaker pole in the water.

As it turned out, the book was to be ours, and at the trophy presentation, Arthur Knapp graciously presented me his classic text *Race Your Boat Right*. The Long Beach Yacht Club now rotates boats each day to foster more even competition.

Four years later, in 1985, with the world match-racing circuit in full swing, I was the only American to compete in all but two of the races (France and Bermuda), and I came up with twenty-nine wins against twelve losses. I placed fifth in the Australia Cup, third in New Zealand, third in Lymington, crewed for Turner in the Congressional Cup, and placed first in the Liberty Cup.

In 1986, I was back in New York for the Liberty Cup, an event that took the spotlight in the city because of its timing. It was held three weeks before the great July 4 harbor festival to celebrate the Statue of Liberty centennial. The backers (the Port Authority of New York and New Jersey) cleverly took advantage of the hoopla over Miss Liberty's birthday party.

New York Harbor is not a stranger to sailboat racing. In fact, before the turn of the century, the America's Cup was raced in its waters, and old photographs show gentlemen and their ladies sitting in deck chairs aboard harbor tugs and steam yachts, observing the races. Like a throwback to those *fin de siècle* days, two McAllister tugs were out with press and VIPs along with a Circle Line tour boat filled with onlookers and a commentator to watch an American crew (us) go against crews from Australia, Sweden, Great Britain, Italy, France, New Zealand, and Japan. It was not necessarily meant as a salute to the French–designed Statue of Liberty, but the boats were French—new, identically rigged Beneteau 305s.

As in many of the match races on the world circuit, the skippers were mainly America's Cup veterans. There was the tall, quiet Colin Beashel of Australia, helmsman of *Australia III* in its sweep of the twelve-meter Worlds in Fremantle, expected to be skipper of the same boat in the America's Cup defense. Yacht designer and boat builder Pelle Pettersen, skipper of the 1977 Swedish challenger *Sverige,* was at the helm of the Swedish entry. Lawrie Smith of Great Britain had been the skipper of the British America's Cup challenger *Victory* in 1983 and helmsman of *Lionheart* in 1980. Mauro Pellaschier had run Italy's *Azzura* in 1983; and Yves Pajot, one of France's top sailors, represented his country.

For us, it was the home court. National as well as personal pride, I think, pushed me toward wanting to win a second time. I had been thinking about the Liberty Cup all year even though I hadn't been racing very much, so I set about organizing my resources. First I recruited a very capable, experienced crew: Jud Smith from Marblehead, Mass., one of the best sail trimmers in the country; Californian Hart Jordan who was with the *Eagle* challenge syndicate; Stu Argo, from Detroit, tailer for the *Heart of America* challenge; and David (Moose) McClintock of Newport, R.I., a premier small-boat racer. Second, I took the time to race in the Lymington Cup, just to get a sense of the match-racing pace again. I came back with a five-won, four-lost record. My English crew had been borrowed, and even though the results were so-so, I felt better about going one-on-one against Pelle Pettersen and Colin Beashel.

I also made an effort to get to New York a few days early to get in some practice, so that when we went out to the line I felt prepared and optimistic about our chances.

The twice-around windward–leeward courses were set between Ellis Island and Liberty Island so that no matter where you were, Miss Liberty loomed. Even more important, we realized very quickly that because of "spring" tides (high-high and low-low), the current was racing between the islands at a speedy clip, about three to four knots, and that was going to be a determining factor in the racing.

The key races for us, as it turned out, were with the Australians. In our first race with Colin Beashel and his crew, the current became an important factor. It was very windy (twenty-five knots), and we became involved in a tacking duel into the current around Ellis

Island. There were so many tacks covering each other that it became obvious we were making no progress on the racecourse. We were simply running in place, the current fixing us in position as if we were on exercise bicycles. Finally we decided to break it off and take a chance on not covering the other boat. I picked a good lift and went out of the current. Suddenly we were making progress on the course, enough to give us a three-boat-length lead on the last windward leg and a win.

After that we had little difficulty in the other races until we came up against the Swedes. Pelle Pettersen is a tough, experienced competitor, and he had a strong crew with him, all of them his own countrymen with the exception of Robby Doyle, who was taking a break from his sailmaking business in Marblehead.

We lost to Pettersen twice—our only losses in the regatta. In the first matchup we thought we had him by a half length after coming from behind, and then we made an elementary mistake: We didn't cover. With a wily racer like Pettersen, you can expect to get bitten with an error like that. Pettersen saw his opportunity, forged ahead, and never looked back.

By Sunday, the last day of racing, our situation could be summed up like this: Our one loss had created two possibilities. If we defeated Pettersen in our second match and won against the Australians, we would automatically win the Liberty Cup. If we lost to the Swedish boat, we still would have to beat the Aussies and hope that the Australians would then take the Swedes, which would give us the win. Of course, if we lost both, I would expect we would see tears in the eyes of the lady on Liberty Island.

There were three races on Sunday. In the first, the

Swedes defeated us handily after we had a bad start and couldn't catch up to them. That put the burden squarely on our crew; the only way to win the Cup now was to wipe out Beashel and crew and then root for them to defeat the Pettersen group.

It took a lot of inner strength to prepare for the match with the Australians. We were angry at ourselves for fouling up on the starting line against the Swedes, but nobody wanted to talk about it. We worked quietly, packed the chute, and got the boat and ourselves organized for the race.

At the start, neither boat had the advantage, and that's the way it stood as we exchanged positions going up the course, Beashel, in his cool way, pushing us to the limit in some very exciting racing—until the second windward mark. At that buoy we both had to do a spinnaker jibe set. Ours was perfect as we rounded the mark. Beashel's crew made one of their few mistakes of the regatta as they wrapped the spinnaker like a pretzel. When the twist was taken out we had an unbreakable three-boat-length lead across the finish line.

Now it was up to the Aussies to redeem themselves and win the regatta for us by beating the Swedes. This time it was Pettersen who made the error at the very start, allowing himself to be pushed over the line early. The Liberty Cup was ours.

If you ever visit the Statue of Liberty, you can see the Cup on display—a five-foot bronze sculpture semicircle with a flat side open in the center, with the shape of a spinnaker in the foreground and the Statue of Liberty in the background.

After it was all over, I remembered how I had struggled back after winning the book that represented last place at the Congressional Cup five years earlier. "Thank you, Arthur Knapp," I said to myself.

THE CHINA SEA RACE:
Just Hang in There

Somehow, Ted Turner convinced me that my offshore racing card needed filling out and that the 650-mile race from Hong Kong to Manila was just the ticket to adventure I had always lacked. Besides, I might even get a Hong Kong suit out of it, something I would always find useful. Turner said all of this in telling me that he had been invited to skipper *Condor* in the race, that he had decided to come out of "retirement" to do it, and that he needed a tactician. "Do you know of one?" he inquired politely.

The challenge was too much to turn down. It was 1984; I was still recovering from participating in the *Defender* defeat at the previous summer's America's Cup, so I flew out to Hong Kong to join *Condor,* a maxiboat, one of a mammoth breed with allowable IOR rating up to seventy feet. Turner had raced the vessel in Australia earlier and was looking forward to another maxiboat matchup with *Nirvana,* the only other big boat in the thirty-seven-boat entry list.

The overwhelming impression of Hong Kong is its throngs of people, many poor refugees from Communist China, who have crowded into this 409-square-mile British Crown Colony that remains the last snippet of the British Empire (at least until 1997). Over five million people live within the boundaries of the colony, and because it is the financial channel between mainland China and the West, you are as apt to see Rolls-Royces and Jaguars on the streets as you are the ubiquitous red Toyota taxis.

No one knows how many people live aboard the sampans that crowd the waterfront, but the harbor itself is full of them, and racing in the local waters has a certain unreal quality that places without sampans do not have. Somehow, they seemed to scatter out of the way of the eighty-plus feet of *Condor* and *Nirvana* as we match-raced in the harbor for a few days before the Hong Kong–Manila race. The Royal Hong Kong Yacht Club sponsors the competition, and the China Sea Race is a vestigial remnant (like the yacht club) of the days when British yachtsmen used the race as a legitimate way of getting to the Philippines for a vacation.

It didn't seem quite like a vacation to me as they loaded several shotguns and an automatic weapon on board along with the provisions. The firearms were there supposedly as a defense against pirates lurking in the South China Sea, although I'm not quite sure what would have happened had we been summoned to "battle stations." Our truly international twenty-eight-member crew, as far as I could tell, had not been welded into a fighting force of Foreign Legion ferocity, although they carried eleven different passports. The prevailing language was English, albeit spoken in several varieties—South African, English, American, Dutch, and German. Of the twenty-eight, there were three Americans: Ted Turner, Mike Turner, and myself.

The international mix of the crew, and its average age, about twenty-seven, reflected how the maxiboats have become magnets for a whole new culture of young sailors who move from vessel to vessel in the same way seamen of Joseph Conrad's time manned tramp steamers. The maxis are attractive because they are the ultimate in big-boat ocean racing. Some are extremely comfortable—noted for their cooking and for comforts such as saunas.

The crew comes together haphazardly. A typical maxiboat passes through Sydney because of the Sydney–Hobart Race. Three people jump on board as crew and stay with the boat. Then the boat goes to Europe, and two more crew members come on board while others leave. You never quite know where the crew members come from, where they are going, how long they will remain on board, or how they earn a living. All are extremely intelligent and cracking good sailors and seamen, doing exactly what they want to do. And that includes having few possessions, no automobile, no mortgage, and a free-and-easy way of life.

Only a few of them were aware of Turner's record; his engineer's cap and his breezy ways were familiar to some of us, but his ability to get the best out of a crew became clear to the others after the first day.

The race began in rain and thirty-knot winds. *Nirvana* flew past *Condor* and after twenty miles left her far behind. With some 630 miles to go it appeared as if we would never catch up. Then Turner called everyone aft for a meeting.

"I don't know how and I don't know when," he said, "but just hang in there, because I guarantee we are going to end up ahead of that boat." He said it with such force and conviction that everyone believed him, wondering how he knew, with *Nirvana* so far ahead, that we could touch her. But it was the Turner way; I had seen it work before, although deep down I had some doubts about his prophecy.

Two days later the sun appeared for the first time, and after a hard reach we found ourselves pulling up to *Nirvana* to the surprised cheers of the crew. With the wind dropping, we pulled ahead of her. Then a tacking duel ensued with the faster *Nirvana* sliding ahead until we would sprint away and end up in the lead. But she would hunt us down and get ahead again in nip-and-tuck crossings that called for the best from our motley group. Finally, an elementary mistake, not covering, allowed *Nirvana* to cross the finish line in Manila Bay first—just beating us by minutes.

Turner congratulated the crew, all of whom had become believers in the power of positive sailing à la Turner. He certainly had me convinced once again, and I've used the technique a number of times since then, exhorting unbelieving crews into having faith in their ability to win.

"I don't know how or where or when," I say, "but we are going to be ahead of this guy. I guarantee it."

THE BERMUDA RACE:
Mind the Meanders

In the pantheon of ocean racing there is one event that ranks as the father of them all. Occurring every two years (on the even-numbered years), the race from Newport, R.I., to Bermuda is an affair that began in 1906, ceased for a few years around the time of World War I, then resumed in 1923 (the one noneven year) to become the most prestigious and best known of all distance races, and the most difficult to enter. Ruled with an iron hand by the Cruising Club of America, which mandates crew experience (half of the crew have to have been in the race before), safety gear, boat configuration, and seaworthiness, the Bermuda Race has been on for so long that its history reads like the story of yacht racing in this country.

Handicapping yachts of different sizes is never easy, but there have been valiant attempts under a number of different rules. Traditionally the race has been a testing ground for offshore designs; for years boats were configured to the CCA's own measurement and handicap rule, and it was relatively recently that the CCA Rule was displaced by the International Offshore Rule (IOR). In fact, to be a Bermuda Race winner is something you can hang with high regard on your personal or business escutcheon. John Alden used his record in the Bermuda race to publicize his designs. His first winners were his Malabar schooners modeled after the husky fishing vessels of the Northeast. Alden was a master at sailing them and scored triple victories in 1923, 1926, and 1930 in *Malabar IV, Malabar VII,* and *Malabar X.*

The grip held by the schooners on ocean racing was dislodged in 1930 by a fifty-two-foot Marconi-rigged yawl named *Dorade,* whose young creator, Olin Stephens, was taking yacht design into a new era. His designs dominated ocean racing for many years to come. *Dorade,* sailed by Olin and brother Rod, took the 1930 Transatlantic Race, which won them a ticker-tape parade when they returned to New York. Stephens's yacht *Edlu,* a development of the slim, long-ended *Dorade,* was the first of many Stephens designs to win the Bermuda Race, in 1934. Twenty-two years later, the thirty-nine-foot centerboarder *Finisterre,* also off the Sparkman and Stephens drafting tables, turned in a remarkable record, her owner, Carleton Mitchell winning three Bermuda races in a row, in 1956, 1958, and 1960. In 1970, more Stephens yachts, Jakob Isbrandtsen's sixty-foot sloop *Running Tide* won Class A while Thomas Watson's *Palawan* and Pat Haggerty's *Bay Bea* monopolized Class B.

In more recent times, the wide-awake CCA, recognizing that there were many ways to skin a rule, opened the race to boats under the relatively new Measurement Handicap System. This effectively splits the fleet between the hot, fast, almost professionally crewed IOR boats and others not entered under IOR who sail with hometown crews. There also is a classic category for yachts of a certain age; in 1986 the famed Stephens-designed *Stormy Weather,* rebuilt at great expense, placed fourth out of thirty-two of her class. Fifty years earlier she had been the winner of the Transatlantic Race.

Like the Fastnet, weather becomes an enormous and often deciding factor in the 630-mile route from Newport to Bermuda. Winds can be light, creating a slow race. But often there are insistent heavy squalls in the Gulf Stream, which the racers have to cross. In 1970, storms and a low-pressure system forced twelve yachts to drop out, seven with dismastings. Ten years earlier, a relatively unforecasted storm caught 135 yachts for more than twenty-four hours with heavy seas and winds that gusted to over sixty knots. It was, up to that time, the largest group of racing boats to be hit in one place simultaneously by severe, potentially life-threatening weather—a record that stood until the 1979 Fastnet disaster.

Bill Robinson, retired editor of *Yachting* magazine, describes in his book *The Sailing Life* what he observed while at the helm of Pierre S. du Pont's famed seventy-two-foot ketch *Barlovento II* during the storm:

The waves tower over us now, rushing out of the black in great looming uneven shapes and with a tumbling crash of crests, I take the first wheel trick.

The biggest problem is vision, with the rain lashing horizontally. I keep my right eye closed and watch the compass with my left . . . the anemometer . . . has never registered below 60 for my whole trick and twice the needle spurts all the way to the top of the dial at 80. It is getting light enough to see the waves now and their reality in the light is worse than the unknown in the darkness. In the worst gusts, the tops are tearing off and blowing straight out. The main never ceases its horrendous rattle, but the skipper sits stoically by as we drive forward.

Despite the weather, the racers kept going, some heaving to for short periods. A tribute, perhaps, to the way boats were built in those days, only three yachts failed to finish, mainly because of damage to their masts. The race was won by *Finisterre,* her third victory in a row. Said Carleton Mitchell, "Thank the Lord for offshore experience."

More than most other distance events, the Bermuda Race is a battle among navigators, the key being the Gulf Stream, that river in the Atlantic that moves with an average speed of three to four knots from the Caribbean along the U.S. coast then across to England. Like all rivers, it has to be forded to get to a destination. A

The maxi yacht *Matador* with large crew on board. *Photographer Sharon Green*

The crew of *Fujimo* looks confused, but actually every man has a specific job to perform. *Photographer Sharon Green*

The crew of *Caiman* climbs the rigging to help heel the boat to get it off the bottom during Cowes Week. *Photographer Guy Gurney*

Cowes Week attracts over eight hundred boats in forty different classes.
Photographer Daniel Forster

Jubilation surfing downwind at the 1984 SORC. When this picture was taken, the air temperature and the wind speed were both thirty-two.
Photographer Sharon Green

Matador was winning this final race in the 1985 Maxi World Championship, but her mast buckled at the final mark and the boat was forced to drop out of the race, giving the championship to *Boomerang*. *Photographer Sharon Green*

Tenacious passes two smaller yachts that had been dismasted in the 1979 Cowes Week. *Photographer Guy Gurney*

Jim Mattingly at the helm of *Tenacious* returning from Fastnet Rock. *Photographer Bud Sutherland*

boat crossing it will be carried downstream for some distance before reaching the other side, so it is easy to understand how important finding the Gulf Stream becomes to the navigator's calculations. All rivers have meanders and back eddies; these are equally important to the progress of a yacht. The uncharted eddies and meanders curl away from the Gulf Stream, moving at a good clip. If you are lucky enough to pick up one moving toward Bermuda, you can catch a ride and move four knots faster than your normal boat speed. A bad eddy can push the boat back home equally as fast.

The navigator has two methods of determining the position of the Gulf Stream and its eddies at any given time. Before the race, infrared satellite photos provided by the U.S. Weather Bureau give a clear picture of the status of the stream for the days preceding the start, providing there is no cloud cover. Once on the course, the navigator's most important instrument, other than Satnav or Loran C (or his sextant), is a thermometer— for the water. Temperatures are constantly taken when the yacht is approaching the Gulf Stream to determine when that line between the cold water of the Atlantic and the warm water of the stream is crossed. There are other signs, too—squalls, warmer air temperature, haze, gulfweed, and sea life. When the Stream is reached, the calculating begins to help make sure the boat is getting a needed lift that can make the big difference at the finish line. Loran and Satnav make a big difference, too: Knowing your precise position allows you to steer more tactically. Your racing fate is less in the hands of the gods.

It was the gods who must have had something to do with my first appearance in the Bermuda Race—an abortive entry as a twenty-four-year-old coach on board a Tripp-designed fifty-four-footer named *Captive* owned by the Merchant Marine Academy. On the first night out, while reefing the roller-furling main, the boom broke and injured one of the crew. We turned around in the fog and powered back some one hundred miles to the coast to get him medical attention.

The 1982 Bermuda Race was one of the fastest in history. The start had been delayed for two days because of a tropical storm spinning across the route. The storm moved away but the residual winds didn't, and aboard George Coumantaros's sixty-five-foot yacht *Boomerang,* we set a spinnaker at the starting line near Newport, took it down an hour later, and close-reached to Bermuda in just sixty-three hours. The winning boat, Marvin Green's eighty-two-foot *Nirvana,* virtually leaped to Bermuda, covering the 650-mile course in two days, fourteen hours, and twenty-nine minutes, breaking the record set by *Ondine* in 1974.

Aboard *Boomerang* we were moving so exhilaratingly fast that we were able to sail the rhumb line (the shortest route), not searching for any extra lift from the Gulf Stream. But in the next Bermuda race in 1984, when I skippered *Jubilation,* the quick currents of the Gulf Stream were a critical factor. Using a meander of the stream was part of the strategy laid out by our navigator, Art Ellis, an experienced one-design sailor with whom I'd raced in the Olympic trials almost eight years earlier.

Getting a good start in a 630-mile distance race may not seem important; by the second night you probably will be alone on the ocean, wondering where the rest of the fleet is. But to me, a good start creates a psychological lift for the crew and sets the mood for keeping the boat moving to its maximum. I knew that we had to achieve that mind-set right from the beginning.

The starting line for the 1984 race was established from a large Coast Guard vessel at the starboard end to the Brenton Reef tower marking port. Nineteen boats were to go to the line in Class A, including *Boomerang* and *Kialoa*. About five minutes before the gun, sailmaker and crew member Mike Toppa, who was trimming the main, turned to me and said, "Gary, if anyone can win this start, you can. Let's go for it."

The windward end was favored by a good fifteen degrees and the class was spread out along the line. I decided to do a timed run, a starting tactic I've used since my collegiate sailing days. Its effectiveness lies in knowing that if you head away from the line for a certain period of time, you know exactly how long it will take to get back. Also, in a timed run, you are using up space to get the boat up to speed. At the end of the run I put the bow down, reaching off five to ten degrees to get up that extra speed to jet ahead of the competition.

Bang. We were across the starting line at full speed right at the committee boat when the gun went off, eliciting a cheer from the spectators and the race committee. It was perfect.

For the first three hundred miles the seas were calm, with a good breeze for high-speed reaching. Then the weather turned sour, with high winds and heavy seas forcing us to strip down to a triple-reefed main and a No. 4 storm jib, which carried us all the way to Bermuda.

But the big trick was finding Art Ellis's pet meander, a stray branch of the Gulf Stream that was heading just where we wanted to go. Art had spotted it on the

NOAA (National Oceanic and Aeronautic Administration) maps; we hit the fast-moving current just right and picked up considerable speed.

It took *Jubilation* ninety-one hours to finish—enough to get us second in Class A. The last thirty miles were the worst; when you know that Bermuda is near and yet so far, the miles no longer tick off so quickly. Finally there was Gibbs Hill and the entrance to St. George's Harbour and the news of our success. But the confinement on the boat wasn't over: Because of her high placement, *Jubilation* had to be inspected and then ferried to Hamilton Harbour to dock with the winners near the pink-and-white Royal Bermuda Yacht Club. Then the parties began and we drank a toast or two to each other and to that unseen but very helpful meander.

THE SOUTHERN OCEAN RACING CONFERENCE:
Looking for an Owner

"It's like a morality play," someone said about the Southern Ocean Racing Conference, "because it has different meanings for different people. Except that it's on the water and seems to take forever, you discover that at SORC things happen at levels beyond your understanding, especially if you are a first-time owner. The SORC, you learn, is no longer for amateurs."

Since its heyday in the 1970s, the SORC, with six races spread out over four weeks, mainly in Florida waters, has become a testing ground for boat design and construction, sail cloth, sail shape, equipment, and electronics to which the ordinary skipper, even a good one with a reasonably fast boat, need not apply. Between November and early February (when the SORC begins), yacht equipment manufacturers are researching and developing new gear they hope might one day take the sailing market by storm. Field-testing begins on the first day of racing, when the SORC contenders come to the starting line in Tampa Bay for a contest in the Gulf of Mexico. But even before that, a tour of the docks at the St. Petersburg Yacht Club is like a boat show in miniature; all of the new stuff and the new boats are there, the company hands present hoping they won't break.

The owner doesn't have to do much searching for crew anymore; if you have a hot boat with a good record, it's likely that (for a price) you may leave the dock with brand-new high-tech sails on board, and a not-so-brand-new sailmaker to make sure they are trimmed right.

This continuing trend has had the effect of diminishing the field. At the height of the SORC's glory in 1973, the fleet contained 140 boats; in 1986, fifty-six vessels were on the starting line for the first race, many of the top ones skippered by the leading pros, myself included. The old idea of the SORC, a "conference" or meeting of amateur racers and their boats, seems to have disappeared in favor of an extension of Grand Prix racing; the pros have taken over, with agendas that may have to do less with racing than with the marketing advantages that come out of success. Dennis Conner said, "The SORC today is more like a convention than it is a regatta, with all the sailmakers, equipment manufacturers, and boatbuilders around who have to have their products tested or introduced. It's still fun, I guess, but it certainly is different."

Still this doesn't diminish the quality or the inherent

dangers of the racing itself. Whenever boats are sent to sea, since Ulysses' time and before, they have to face the vagaries of nature. And the SORC, even though it doesn't include major offshore long-distance races such as Newport–Bermuda, or the Fastnet, has had its share of difficulties. There have been beachings, sinkings, and even deaths; the ocean has shown no quarter to pros and amateurs alike.

I have been in the SORC thirteen times, and one of the several occasions I have been happy to return to the dock was in 1979, after twenty-two hours of hard racing aboard *Tenacious* in the Ocean Triangle, one of the sextet of races that has made up the SORC circuit. The 160-mile competition started at Miami; went around Great Isaac Light, which marks the entrance to the central Bahamas and its minefield of reefs; then proceeded northwest to Palm Beach and back to Miami. The race started in a twenty-five-knot norther, typical for Florida at that time of year, and by the time the fleet began crossing the Gulf Stream, which is just offshore, seas were breaking between ten and twelve feet.

Our boom snapped in half thirty minutes after the start. A jury-rigged spinnaker pole allowed us to sheet the main reasonably well. Then, an hour later, the head of the spinnaker blew out. Luckily the wind was blowing so hard we were able to get the sail on board before it became trapped under the hull. After an exhausting seventy-five-mile beat from Great Isaac Light to Palm Beach, the mainsail ripped in half twenty feet down from the top, from leech to luff. For the final two hours of the race, including a windward mark rounding and a spinnaker set for the final reach to the Miami sea buoy, we sailed without the main.

Badly as we were bruised and deck gear on the boat

damaged, worse news came when we docked. A crewman off Pirana had been lost at sea. He had been standing near the stern, apparently lost his hold, and tumbled into the water. He was kept in sight while a second crewman, on a line, went in after him. After ten minutes of struggling in the heavy seas to get the first crewman on board, he slipped away and disappeared, presumably drowned. His death was the second to plague that particular SORC. During the extremely windy St. Petersburg–Ft. Lauderdale Race a week earlier, a crewman on *Obsession,* a forty-six-foot sloop, had died after being hit on the head by the boom during an accidental jibe. The crew struggled to revive him, but to no avail.

Heroism also has played a part in SORC history. In the 1974 Miami–Nassau race, the yacht *Winoweh* miscalculated her position at night and ran afoul of a reef near Great Isaac. Another participant in the race, the yacht *Osprey,* rescued the entire crew and went on to the finish. Ironically, when the extra time that *Osprey* had spent in the rescue effort was subtracted from her elapsed time, she ended up as the Miami–Nassau winner.

Another potential disaster, in the 1975 SORC, was averted by superb seamanship and teamwork. The forty-foot Standfast sloop *Mary E.* was leading her class in a forty-knot gale that was whipping up twelve-foot Gulf Stream seas when she began to founder fourteen miles west of Great Isaac. First on the scene was a Carter 39, *Phoenix,* which managed to get a line aboard the *Mary E.,* winch the two boats together, and take off three members of the crew before the line parted and the two boats separated. Next to arrive was the sloop *J&B,* coskippered by Mort Engel and sailmaker Jack Sutphen. Engel suggested that the crew of the *Mary E.* remove a submersible strobe light from one of the personal harnesses, attach it to a halyard, and raise it to the top of the mast to mark the boat's position; she was virtually invisible in the storm. Other boats were able to join in the rescue effort. The rescue took eight hours until the entire crew of the *Mary E.* had been taken off through the use of an inflatable dinghy. The *J&B* continued on to Nassau, leaving a Coast Guard cutter on the scene to watch the *Mary E.* go down. It was felt that the keel of the *Mary E.* had come loose because of the severe wave action, opening the hull to the sea.

Competing in SORC opened my eyes and my senses to big-boat, big-time racing, although in the first few years I was generally in misery because of a tendency to seasickness.

In 1973, I sailed the St. Petersburg–Ft. Lauderdale race aboard a C&C 39 named *Checkmate.* I was twenty-two and had been named Collegiate Sailor of the Year, but all my racing was in one-design dinghies, and I felt in awe of the crew on board *Checkmate.* We did not do well, and I wondered if it was because of my inexperience or if perhaps I was out of my league.

The next year I came back on another C&C 39. They were the hot racing boats in a time when production craft, albeit modified, still could compete and do well. For the next three years I joined Art Wullschlager's noted *Golliwog* with Graham Hall as skipper but didn't sail in all the circuits. The first year aboard (1974) I had my first stint as watch captain, doing a great deal of the steering and we finished second in Class D.

Then I sailed on a C&C 43 in 1975, losing only to *Charisma* and *Tenacious,* now owned by Turner. In 1976 I sailed on another Wullschlager boat, *Fire One,* a new

Doug Peterson-designed Two-Tonner, and we were third in Class D.

From 1973 to 1976 I took part in four different circuits on four different boats, and still I didn't feel that I understood big-boat ocean racing. It wasn't until the following year, when I joined Turner and spent four years aboard *Tenacious,* that I began to grasp offshore racing.

I learned how to take any series of maneuvers—spinnaker sets, tacking, jibes, jibe sets, and the like—and break them down to their component parts. I learned when to do these maneuvers and when not to. I learned what combinations of sails to use and how long to keep them up, which was one of Turner's fortes.

Even though I served as Turner's tactician and main helmsman, I felt I was going through an apprenticeship in ocean racing, absorbing things even as simple as removing wet foul-weather gear before going below. I also began to have a feel for managing a crew.

In retrospect, Turner and *Tenacious* were my teachers in learning the art of helmsmanship and working with the sail trimmers. Aboard a Turner boat, you were meant to concentrate while at the wheel, or you were relieved from the helm. I learned that if you weren't using the trimmers to keep the boat moving efficiently, you were not steering well. Now I always make it a point to spend at least 40 percent of every race at the helm, because of the experience I gain in boathandling in every sort of condition.

Concentration, that was the key. I learned not to be distracted by what was happening on deck and to concentrate on two important criteria—angle of heel and what the wind is apt to do next—and to feed that information to the sail trimmers. Aboard *Tenacious* we trimmed on every wave to keep the boat going. The commands were constant. "Traveler up . . . traveler down. Leads inboard . . . outboard . . . forward . . . aft. Jib in . . . jib out. Okay, ease halyard tension." No resting for the trimmers and least of all for the helmsman, and for that matter, for the rest of the crew. It was a game of inches, and we tried to get *Tenacious* to do impossible things. But it paid off. In four years of racing in the circuit, we had two firsts and two seconds in Class A in magnificent battles with Al Van Metre's *Running Tide*—a close sister ship to *Tenacious*. For four years we swapped places with *Tide;* the boat that won seemed to be the vessel with the newer sails.

Now, after thirteen years of sailing in the SORC, I find the changes are very noticeable: The time span of the circuit makes it too expensive for anyone but professionals to participate. The period of racing should be shortened to a maximum of two weeks.

Racing in the circuit is no longer fun. If you ask participants, "Do you enjoy the SORC?" the answer probably will be, "No, I don't enjoy it. It's strictly business for me."

Crews having become very unfriendly, refusing to talk about their vessels. Rafting up at the docks, common at the sponsoring yacht clubs, no longer happens. Owners, in fact, go to considerable lengths to avoid being part of the crowd by dispersing to the local marinas.

There is too little racing for the amount of effort involved. The longer races leave too much to chance. When the wind increases, small boats win; when it decreases, big boats win. A fairer test would be to de-emphasize the longer races (the St. Petersburg–Ft. Lauderdale Race now counts 27 percent) and give the shorter races more weight. Day races of thirty to fifty miles in length would be a good test of skills, since the wind normally doesn't change in a four- to six-hour period, and the competition would be fairer. Finally, the courses need to be more creative to put more emphasis on tactics.

It may be that understanding the changes yacht racing has been undergoing as well as a little creative thinking will restore the SORC to its glory days, when a visitor heard the welcome call, "C'mon on board and have a beer. Is there anything you'd like to see?"

It'll be the owner talking.

HALL OF FAME REGATTA:
No Names, Please

Imagine sailing in a race against fifteen of the world's best and most famous sailors, not only your contemporaries, but also the stars of the past twenty years. Imagine, here are your heroes—men whose books have been your bibles since childhood, others whom you have always admired but never met—on the same starting line with you. The faces around you are all intense on tactics and sailing well, and you can't help wondering how you came to be in this nightmarish position.

In 1982, I was in this position as the result of a scheme sponsored by *Yacht Racing/Cruising* magazine to celebrate its twentieth anniversary. The magazine solicited its readers to nominate the top twenty sailors of the past two decades. The twenty were named to the *Yacht Racing* Hall of Fame and were invited to compete against each other in a regatta in Newport, R.I. Fifteen accepted. I was surprised and honored to be included in the group, and I signed up for the regatta, although the prospects for success were unclear. After all, here was a group of sailors who collectively had won sixty-two world championships and collected eleven Olympic medals and more than two hundred national sailing titles. Four had defended the America's Cup, and nine of the fifteen who sailed in the event had competed in the Olympics. Of the top twenty picked by the readers, two had passed away—Uffa Fox and Sir Francis Chichester. Three others—Tom Blackaller, Ted Turner, and Ted Hood—had other commitments. So we were left with, unbelievably, Arthur Knapp, Jr.; Paul Elvstrom; George O'Day; and Stuart Walker, expert racers as well as theoreticians. Among my peers were Dave Ullman, John Bertrand, and Dennis Conner. Buddy Melges was there, and so were Hobie Alter, Lowell North, and dinghy racer Steve Benjamin. Rounding out the field were Bob Bavier and, surprisingly, Eric Tabarly of France, pausing long enough between long-distance ocean-racing events to come to Newport. It was a remarkable array of talent—racing skills combined with seminal influence on the sport. A whole breed of young French ocean competitors had grown up under Tabarly's tutelage. And by now I certainly knew Arthur Knapp's book *Race Your Boat Right* very well.

I was involved with *Defender* that summer, but I decided I wanted to win the regatta. The race was to be held in Etchells 22s, a spirited one-design boat that is widely used in the Northeast, so I began recruiting the two best crews I could find. Etchells champion Dave Curtis, of Marblehead, was unavailable, but he suggested his cohort, Jud Smith. "I got a guy who is the best Etchells sailor around," Curtis said. "If you take him, you'll win." So Smith was signed up. And so was Hank Stuart of Ithaca, N.Y., a very aggressive, all-around sailor who has the knack of easing the tension on a skipper.

On the first morning, we were able to get an hour of practice on what turned out, by the luck of the draw, to be the slowest boat in the fleet. (Boats were rotated each day.) The tune-up seemed to be going well in light air. But seeing the other members of the fleet working around the buoys in Newport Harbor, practicing tacks and spinnaker sets and jibes, I suddenly had a sinking feeling: What if I'm last against these people—Lowell North and Dennis Conner and Buddy Melges and Paul Elvstrom, and the others?

But then I got active. I began maneuvering for the start, and all my training and experience and ability focused on the moment. This was no time for internal doubt. Something had clicked, and I no longer cared who my competitors were. Very strangely, my mind reverted back to a familiar setting—collegiate racing. I was up against other college sailors in Etchells 22s, I was twenty years old again, and I was going to be very aggressive. Going for it at the start, with twenty-five seconds to go, I found a big hole in the middle of the line of boats and slid into it. Then I port-tacked the fleet, moving quickly to the right side of the course.

We began moving ahead, and the butterflies came back as Stuart yelled, "We've got Melges by half a boat length, and we're crossing Conner!" I replied, "No names. Just give me the sail numbers."

Then Jud Smith suggested something brilliant. He said, "Ease the backstay a quarter of an inch." I did that and took the mainsheet out of its cam cleat, letting one tooth go by, and put the mainsheet back in. Jud was trimming the jib, and his eyes never left his work as he said, "That's better now."

I was instantly calm. I thought, if he can tell, with that minute easing of the mainsheet, that it did the jib good, we'll be in great shape. And we were.

We overshot the windward mark in that first race and went from first to fourth at the finish line. Among our cheerleaders was Graham Hall, who had been my coach at the New York Maritime College. Here's how Roger Vaughan, in *Sail,* described Hall's reaction after we won the second race: "Jobson's boat was approached by a launch carrying Graham Hall and a videotape crew. A great shout from the launch echoed across the water: "hey,Hey,HEY!" It was the exuberant, guttural call invented by comic Bill Cosby to signify the heavy-footed approach of his character Fat Albert. . . . 'At New York Maritime,' Hall said later, 'whenever someone did well in a race the team would give him the old Fat Albert call to pump him up.' "

We took a third and two seconds in the succeeding days and won the regatta. It was one of the great moments in my life—equal to being named Barnegat Bay Sailor of the Year as a high-school kid sixteen years earlier. Sitting in the Etchells after an exhausting last race in which we placed second and knew we had won the regatta, we again heard from the videolaunch, "hey, Hey, HEY!"

In the standings we were followed by Buddy Melges and Dave Ullman, then by Paul Elvstrom, the tough, bearded Dane who had been the No. 1 vote-getter in the readers' poll. Surprisingly, Arthur Knapp came in fifth; he was seventy-five at the time and told everyone, "If my doctor knew I was here, he would raise hell."

After it was over, Melges, always a gentleman, said, "I thought about getting mean and really dogging Gary and taking him to the back of the fleet where I would have a better chance to put him away. But what the heck. We came here to have fun."

3

PLACES: A LIFE ON THE WATER

*F*or those of us who make their living in the sport of sailing, our haunts are the great harbors and bays we sail out of from time to time in competition with our peers to get to the next harbor first. We frequent Long Island Sound and Chesapeake Bay, Narragansett Bay and Block Island Sound, San Francisco Bay, Long Beach, the Solent, and Fremantle. "Have seabag, will travel" is our motto as we fly from one place to another. In a period of a week in June 1986, I competed in New York Harbor in the Liberty Cup; then, on the evening of the last race, I flew a chartered plane to Block Island and spent four days participating in Block Island Race Week. Thursday and Friday found me in Connecticut recording voice-overs for ESPN, Saturday morning in Marblehead, Mass., from where I drove to Boston's Logan International Airport to catch a flight to California. There I would sail in Santa Cruz with Buddy Melges and the midwestern American's Cup challenger *Heart of America*.

Cities are not for us. We are as attached to the water as the early voyagers were. Perhaps it is true, as researchers have pointed out, that there is in some of us a "Ulysses complex" that drives us to the sea, stronger in some than in others, stronger among single-handers and round-the-world passagemakers and live-aboard cruising folk, perhaps, than in ocean racers. If we are all descendants of primordial amphibians, than maybe a few cells of those ancient animals remain in some of us and have the power to whisper that the sea is our real home.

It's not surprising then, that while we didn't choose where we grow up and are first taught about boats and the nautical life, we do have something to say about where we choose to go to school and where we go to conduct our business and, most of all, where we find a home port and a safe harbor, a place to return to amid the rushing from one place to another.

The most significant places in my life have all been associated with the water: Barnegat Bay, N.J., where I grew up and first began racing; Long Island Sound, where I passed my collegiate racing years; Newport, R.I., where an inordinate amount of time was spent learning the America's Cup game; Chesapeake Bay and its sailing capital, Annapolis, where I live now and that is the home port and safe harbor I always hoped to have.

In the spring of 1977, prior to the America's Cup, while *Courageous* was being tested in the waters off Marblehead, I spent many of my off-hours walking through the streets and byways of this 350-year-old

Massachusetts town. Marblehead is on an ancient gla-
cial peninsula that juts northeast into the Atlantic Ocean.
It is a place very much of the sea, its rocky, steep fore-
shore swept by ten-foot tides. Many evenings at sunset
I would stand on the headland in the town's little park
at Fort Sewall and look toward Cape Ann, dimly visi-
ble to the northeast in the fading light. There would
be a lobster boat heading back into the harbor, or a
sailboat endeavoring to get home before dark, and the
view would be comforting. I understood, then, I think,
why I had chosen the water and its environment to
work and live in. The late British writer Nicholas
Monsarrat expressed it even more clearly:

> Let me end my days somewhere where the tide
> comes in and out; leaving its tribute, its riches,
> taking nothing. Giving all the time: pieces of wood,
> pieces of eight, seaweed for the land, logs for the
> fire, sea-shells for pleasure, skeletons for sadness.

BARNEGAT BAY:
Where the Pines Meet the Sea

One of the unique features of the U.S. East Coast is
the chain of barrier islands and captive bays that ex-
tends from Down East Maine to Florida. One of these
is Barnegat Bay, a fifty-six-mile stretch of mainly shallow water that reaches along the New Jersey shore from
Bay Head and Manasquan Inlet south to Brigantine,
just above Atlantic City. On the outside, the bay is

protected from the Atlantic Ocean by barrier beaches such as Island Beach and Long Beach Island. There are only a few natural passages between the ocean and the bay, mainly twisted inlets with shifting sands that drive the U.S. Coast Guard crazy trying to place buoys to keep boats from going aground. One of these, Barnegat Inlet, is notorious for its dogleg channel, which, from the outside, makes it appear as if vessels will be beached before they get inside. The New Jersey inlets are notoriously treacherous, too, in times of bad weather and heavy surf. It is a fragile area, overgrown now by beach communities and condominiums and shopping centers. It's easy, under the weight of asphalt roads and too many buildings, to misunderstand how fragile these islands really are until Mother Nature strikes back. Hurricanes have devastated the islands since before there were written records. In more recent years, a storm in the Northeast overwhelmed Long Beach Island and created an inlet where none existed, carrying away an entire beach community named Harvey Cedars along with it.

Inside the bay, the ecology of the mainland is equally fragile, and land is becoming just as overdeveloped as the islands. The mainland has salt marsh and pine barrens, an immense tract that is the last of its kind in the United States and where rivers such as the Mullica run red, colored by the bog iron in the soil. The developers want this land, too, and once there was even the possibility that a new international airport for the metropolitan corridor might be built there, an idea that people seemed to realize was so mistaken that it finally died.

It is an area rich with natural life. The Brigantine National Wildlife Refuge at the southern end of Barnegat Bay is the winter home of a species of small northern goose called brant, which summers in the Arctic and congregates in the eelgrass of the bay in winter. Once there were so many brant that a town along the bay was named after them.

Because of the solitude along the mainland shore and the beautiful island beaches, the area had always been a summer place for Philadelphians and New Jerseyites. If you had some money you built a large summer house in Bay Head or Seaside Park or Toms River. If you were like my father's family, you were content with summer cottages along the sleepy mainland shore of the bay centered around a sailing club.

This was Beachwood, where, in the days before the Second World War, if you subscribed to the *Philadelphia Inquirer,* you could buy a piece of property in the summer colony at a reduced rate. My father's family always had vacationed there, and when he returned from serving in the Marines, he and my mother moved from northern New Jersey to nearby Toms River. He had accepted a job on the *Asbury Park Press,* and as he loved to sail and had been involved with the Beachwood Yacht Club, the move seemed the sensible thing to do.

New England and Long Island Sound may be considered by some to be the sailing centers of the East Coast, but in Barnegat Bay and, indeed, all along the New Jersey shore, people think differently. Barnegat Bay, the Shrewsbury River, and places such as Red Bank and Rumson are their sailing haunts. On Barnegat Bay, because it is so shallow, a local boat, the sneakbox, was developed in the 1920s. Gaff-rigged and fifteen to seventeen feet long, with swept-back centerboards, they reigned supreme on Barnegat Bay for a long time.

My great-aunt on my father's side, Frances Wemple, was one of the best sailors on the bay, according to family tradition. Beachwood before the war was known as the Polyhue Yacht Club because each member had a different-colored sail. Families would take the train down from Jersey City or Newark or up from Philadelphia for the weekend or for vacations, and they would race sneakboxes. Great-aunt Frances was famous for her sail, which was dyed scarlet; the sail must have struck terror into the hearts of her opponents, because she won everything. My mother had a nautical heritage as well. She didn't sail, but she came from a seafaring family in Rehoboth, Delaware, with several ship captains among her ancestors.

This was the environment in which I grew up, sailing and Beachwood being integral parts of my life. The yacht club was nothing special, especially compared to the "rich" ones around the bay. It had no heat and wasn't insulated, but it had a lot of hot, scrappy sailors and a junior sailing program with 150 kids in it.

I was six years old when I first began sailing, and I distinctly remember disliking the "low side," even when I day-sailed around the bay with my father or did an overnight with him on one of the series of boats we owned. When we overnighted, we might visit another yacht club and then anchor in a nearby cove where the pines came down to the beach "to meet the sea," as they said locally. Cruising Barnegat Bay was not always a pleasure, however. One Friday evening when we visited the Shore Acres Yacht Club, the bar was in full swing, and so were the mosquitoes. New Jersey's mosquitoes are particularly vicious; they were not amiable that night and literally rained on us when we went back to the boat to sleep.

My first regatta took place about the same time. If you were a little kid (I was the skinniest one around), you had one job on the leaky Barnegat Bay sneak-boxes. You stood up and bailed all of the way around the course. And that is the way the summers flowed all through my childhood and young adolescent years. Sailing was something you automatically did when school ended, just like you played touch football or ice hockey during the winter.

On Barnegat Bay, the sport was a well-organized activity. During the week you had sailing lessons or practiced racing every day. On the weekends, the Barnegat Bay Racing Association held competitions on Saturday, with the race committee always out in full regalia of white ducks, blue blazers, and yachting caps. On Sunday you raced at your own club. So as I grew older, the standard routine for me was participating in the bay races on Saturday at any one of the ten clubs that hosted regattas during the summer. In the morning most of the kids would sail the Penguins, sneak-boxes, and M-scows, and then in the afternoon the breeze would come up and the adults would race the E-scows and the A-cats and the Sanderlings. If you were good enough, you might crew for them.

For me, however, sailing competition began to take up a significant part of my time, with summer racing extending into winter frostbiting. It wasn't something my father encouraged, even though he had been commodore of the Beachwood Yacht Club; he wanted us to be well rounded in sports, and I had been just as happy with competitive wrestling while in high school as I was with sailing.

One day, on Barnegat Bay, perhaps while crewing for Sam Merrick (now former head of the Olympic sailing program) or while in the heat of solo competition, I decided that I would do whatever it took to get into the sailing life. That year the men in blue blazers and white ducks named me Outstanding Junior Sailor of the Year. I felt I had paid my dues to the bay that had nurtured me, and soon it would be time to move on.

LONG ISLAND SOUND:
The View from (Under) the Bridge

Sometime around the end of December 1970, I wrote an insistent note to myself in one of the logbooks I kept in those days:

1. Set goal high.
2. Aggressive attack.
3. Progressive organization.
4. Take it as it comes, but keep plugging.
5. All-out—never halfway.
6. Never give in.
7. Nice guys finish last. Within the spirit of the rules, be hard-nosed. Use the rules to advantage.

I don't recall what brought this on. Perhaps I had become too intense about racing—a stringbean of a post-adolescent with crewcut hair, living in the regimented environment of New York Maritime College at Fort Schuyler, at the very western end of Long Island Sound. After the freedom of Barnegat Bay, it was not the kind of world I was used to, and maybe racing represented a way in which I could control my own destiny.

I certainly did a lot of racing. Between 1969, when I enrolled at Fort Schuyler, and the end of my third year of college in 1971, I spent 351 days on the water, taking part in 921 races. I logged every race—wind and weather conditions, starts, strategy, members of the crew, type of boat. What seems significant, looking back, is that I was obsessed with numbers, totaling days raced and wins and losses.

In fact, I was so wound up that I was not racing well, protesting, nervous, losing more than I was winning. Graham Hall pointed out that unless I went out and had fun, I wasn't going to make it. Graham was right. Once I started racing for fun, the nervousness dropped away and I started winning again and, in fact, was named Collegiate All-American three times as well as the outstanding College Sailor of the year in 1972 and 1973.

Graham Hall's reputation had brought me to New York Maritime in the first place. I had decided that one way or another, sailing was going to be a very important part of my life, and this meant going to a college with a strong sailing program. The Ivy League schools were out of the question, and when Dick Curry, for whom I was crewing, talked about Hall's record at the U.S. Naval Academy (six national titles) and what he was planning at New York Maritime, it seemed an ideal solution. The idea of being schooled as a merchant marine officer also had intrinsic appeal. I could obtain a college degree, get professional nautical training, and race, all at the same time.

New York Maritime, part of the state university system, does not have one of your more elegant campuses. The school is on Throgs Neck, a peninsula in the Bronx that juts into Eastchester Bay, a body of water that separates the Bronx on the north from City Island and the upper reaches of New York City to the south. It's the part of Long Island Sound that empties into the East River, like water flowing out of the neck of a very large jug. Fort Schuyler, which houses the college in a pentagon of old gray stone buildings erected in 1830, was designed, in fact, to protect New York City from sea attack from the sound. A century later officials, in their wisdom, decided to open the city to vehicular attack from the north and built the Throgs Neck Bridge between the Bronx and Queens, leaving Fort Schuyler in its shadow.

The bridge loomed big in our lives; we sailed under it and took cognizance of the currents in and around it. We had adventures directly related to the bridge. In March 1970, a friend and I went sailing on one of the college's Skipjacks on a very windy day. We planed back and forth across the entrance to the East River and found ourselves on the leeward shore close to the Queens end of the bridge, where we capsized. The water was cold, the afternoon was waning, and we hung on to the bottom of the boat until a New York City police boat came along and put a line around our mast and towed us to shore. To add to our embarrassment, a police helicopter hovered nearby, although it wasn't used.

We pulled the boat up on the beach and a police car very obligingly drove us back to the college, taking an hour to cross the bridge in rush-hour traffic. When we arrived at the college, there was Hall and some members of the sailing team waiting for us, obviously worried about our disappearance. It taught us a lesson— always to call coaches, wives, family upon return if there has been a departure from the norm while sailing.

My introduction to the Maritime College sailing program provided my first experience on a big boat. In June 1969, having been accepted at Fort Schuyler, I was invited to join the crew of the college's offshore racing boat, *Resistance,* a forty-two-foot Comanche, for the Annapolis–Newport race.

For an eighteen-year-old who had never sailed anything over thirty feet and had hardly ever been away from Barnegat Bay, the experience of being on my first long big boat race was an eye-opener. The race turned out to be one of those affairs in which the weather becomes one of the competitors: Heavy rain, line squalls, heat, and calms were instrumental in slowing the 3½-day race to five days. I spent five days draped over the rail when off watch and at the helm when on. The boat had a tiller and a hiking stick, and I found that I enjoyed steering a big boat—that I seemed to have a knack for it.

We arrived in Newport at 3:00 A.M. with time during the dawn hours to get a brief look at the town, to stroll down Thames Street looking at the photos of the America's Cup yachts in the windows of the shops, and, at 8:00 A.M., to catch a bus home to Toms River.

I had not realized that Long Island Sound is one of the great boating centers of the nation and a hotbed of yacht racing until I entered Fort Schuyler that fall and began competing. I had never seen so many boats congregated in one area and so many racing possibilities. The Coast Guard, in 1971, estimated that there were 250,000 boats registered around the perimeter of the sound and that about ten thousand of them might be under way at any given time. Jules Wilensky, in the fourth edition of his boating guide to Long Island Sound, said: "Add small unregistered sailboats, trailered boats, and commercial traffic and you begin to see why Long Island Sound's 1,300 square miles comprises the busiest boating area in the nation."

Wilensky also had something to say about racing: "There has been a phenomenal growth in class sailboat racing. . . . During Larchmont Race week, the boats are so thick on the water, it seems possible to walk across the Sound on them. Stamford Yacht Club starts more than 100 boats in the Vineyard Race Labor Day weekend."

Wilensky didn't know the half of it. There was more racing on Long Island Sound than I could have imagined. On weekends, there was club racing at every one of the hundred or so yacht clubs that dot the sound. There were big boat events using marks in the sound itself, and dinghy racing in any one of a dozen classes in every harbor along the northern shore of Long Island and the southern shore of New York and Connecticut. This was the area, after all, that had controlled racing for a long time and whose yachtsmen raced the twelve-meter and offshore yachts. In 1967, all four of the U.S. twelve-meters entered in the challenger trials were skippered by Long Island Sound yachtsmen, although one of them, Briggs Cunningham, later migrated to California.

These men came from ancient and honorable yacht clubs on the sound where status was important. On Barnegat Bay there was not much difference among the yacht clubs, although some drew from a wealthier clientele. But no matter what your background and social standing, you were treated equally at each club.

Between our collegiate races we were invited to the Long Island Sound clubs to participate in their regattas individually, or as a team. I was never really comfortable in the hallowed halls of some of the clubs; we felt in some way imperfect with our crewcut hair and tattered foul-weather gear when confronted with the perfect young people we raced against with their perfect boats and perfect sweaters and just the right boat shoes. We made it a point of honor to show them on the course just how good we were.

Typical of the places we returned to after a race was the Larchmont Yacht Club, (now 106 years old), a huge, regal, wooden building with an enormous veranda facing the sound. Joseph Cooper, in his book *Land's End Water's Edge,* describes the interior we found when we arrived for the Shields Nationals in 1970:

> Through the main door is the lobby, which alone houses enough nautical memorabilia to make a New England antique dealer swoon. To the right, an oil painting of the Atlantic seems to stretch out across the wall from the doorsill to the reception desk. Across the room, brass cannons guard the fireplace whose mantel is decked with yacht racing treasures from days when even our coins were made of silver.
>
> Passing on either side of the fireplace, one enters the Club's Tap Room, or grill, and the adjoining bar. Surrounding the bar on three sides and forming the westernmost portion of the main clubhouse is an enclosed porch. Half-hull models . . . are mounted at the top of all three interior walls with old photographs, drawings and clippings hung below.

Cool as we tried to be, my crew and I were overwhelmed—so much so, I think, that we allowed ourselves to be psyched on the course on the first two races of the five that were held. There were forty-two Shields in the regatta, representing the best crews in the nation. Our crew that day included coach Hall, and there was no reason why we shouldn't have done well. In the first race we placed twenty-sixth. My log showed that we had a good start about halfway down the line, but we lost ground taking fliers and then made it up by beating boats downwind and on the last weather leg.

In the second race that day, I was over the line six seconds early after a general recall and had to go around the committee boat again. "Poor judgment and current pushed me over," I wrote. Still, we finished fifteenth. On the way back to the dock, Hall announced, "I won't be here tomorrow, so take over. Just relax." Without Hall around to guide us we were uncomfortable that evening; we seemed not to have the right kind of clothes for dinner at the yacht club, although we went anyway.

We may have been uncomfortable at dinner, but we didn't show it on the ten-mile Gold Cup course the following day. My notes for the third race indicate that we were much more relaxed:

"New day. Good start at leeward end. Last boat to tack for mark and were 2nd around and moved into 1st. Stayed in the lead the whole way until another boat took a flier in the last leeward leg and beat us on a shift. Finished 2."

We placed second in the fourth race by calling the right wind shifts, and in the last race placed twenty-fifth after overshooting a windward mark in a "slow, wide rounding."

Still, I was learning my trade. After the regatta (we placed tenth overall), I wrote:

"Shields fun to sail to weather. Slow off the wind.

Have to think in terms of where to go. Start in clear air on right side and you win easy. Downwind get chute going. Jibe if possible, keep air clear and play angles. Trick is to know where to go."

It wasn't clear to me how much I had learned from the constant racing and coaching until I went home to Barnegat Bay on my first vacation and entered a Penguin regatta in my own boat—the same Penguin I had been racing in for years. There were thirty-five boats in the fleet, and all conditions were the same as they had been every summer. I had been struggling when I left, but on this day I won every race, something I had never done before.

Long Island Sound had done its work. I had become a student of the sport. I knew I could face up to anyone on any course in most boats. But there was a lot more to learn, and I was going to "keep plugging."

NEWPORT, R.I.:
Terminally Addictive

In 1644, the dissident religious leader Roger Williams, who is considered the founder of Rhode Island, obtained a patent from the King of England uniting Newport and neighboring Portsmouth with his Providence colonies under the banner of complete political and religious freedom. Since then, Newport, at various times, has been a haven for the persecuted, a wealthy seaport in the "triangle" trade (molasses, rum, and slaves), an almost private resort for the overwhelmingly wealthy, a Navy town, a yachting community, and more recently a tourist mecca where you can buy fake scrimshaw, have a very expensive room with a harbor view, and bet a few dollars at the (legal) jai-alai fronton.

We mention all of these things because it offers some idea of the many sides of this town of some thirty thousand people on Aquidneck Island on the eastern side of Narragansett Bay, not far from the Sakonnet River. Belted by a semi-industrial area of modest houses, businesses, and shopping centers like most other New England towns, it isn't until you penetrate to the heart of the matter—the waterfront and the Revolutionary War Hill and Point sections—that you begin to have some idea of Newport's attractiveness.

The people who work, eat, and sleep in Newport constitute several different populations, which hardly ever come together except in conducting the day's business. First, there are those who service the community, the gas station attendants and the storekeepers and the supermarket checkers. Add the lobstermen and fishing trawler crews and the boatbuilders and yardworkers. Then there are those who are served, the very rich (Norris D. Hoyt's term), tourists, transient yachtsmen, and practically anyone else engaged in some intellectual pursuit. The military population (mostly Navy) stands alone at its base north of Newport, with the Naval War College and other facilities much shrunken from the times not long ago when Newport was considered a "Navy town," with its destroyer squadron and torpedo base and suitable facilities downtown to entertain the sailors.

Norris Hoyt, sailor, writer, and raconteur, and a noted chronicler of Newport life, has written:

As one of the happy few residing in what Long-
fellow called, "the city by the sea," I assume that
to most people the name Newport conjures up
images of Mrs. Astor's mounted dinner parties for
her horse, Ted Turner aboard *Courageous* stalking
Australia with intent to triumph, the U.S. Navy
War College simulating micro-miniaturized Ar-
mageddon in a former insane asylum. . . . Actually we regard our activities as normal but normal
in a special way. With the America's Cup, the
Tennis Hall of Fame, the Bermuda Race, the
American Jumping Derby, the Olympic sailing
trials, the mansions, Historic Hill, we expect to be
viewed with wonder as we do our daily rising,
working, eating and sleeping.

The yachting population has its own subgroups. First
there are the local sailors, who may be members of one
of the three yacht clubs (Ida Lewis, Newport, or Navy),
or may just have a mooring or a dock space and stay
away from organized sailing. Members of the yacht
profession also abound in Newport because it's a nice
place to be if you are a sailmaker or yacht designer or
a builder or racing crew member, run someone's boat
or would like to. Those who run boats are called captains; the powerboat captains can be identified by their
freshly pressed khakis (boats under a hundred feet) or
whites (boats over a hundred feet). The sailboat captains uniformly wear polo shirts (white or navy) with
the name of the boat over the left pocket, khaki shorts,
and boat moccasins without socks. A real pro working
around the boat wears over the right hip a holster that
contains a rigging knife, pliers, and a marlinspike.
A third group, the yachting transients, also can be

divided into two categories: vacationing sailors who are having a nice time working their way along the coast individually, and vacationing sailors who find it fun to take part in their yacht club's annual cruise. If you are a member of the New York Yacht Club, the latter kind of cruising is very proper, with appropriate signal flags flown by the commodore, appropriate dress, sunset gun, and the like. Newport always has been a port of call for the NYYC; so much so that at one time the club had a Newport Station on one of the wharves. It's now a restaurant, but some of the old plaques and pictures still are there. The New York Yacht Club now uses the Ida Lewis Yacht Club as a station.

On this setting superimpose a flood of several thousand vacationers out for a good time and you get some idea of Newport during an America's Cup summer. What they have come to see and perhaps touch and be part of is out of reach: a small colony of talented sailors; their technicians, handlers, and front men and their boats; and the twelve-meter yachts that hang suspended in their cradles in off-limits boatyards when they are not out sailing.

The closest they can come to this mysterious world is to gather in front of the press headquarters in the town's armory on Thames Street, hoping that someone important (Turner, Conner?) will emerge. "Is that anybody?" they ask a magazine editor.

I knew nothing of the America's Cup scene—or of Newport, for that matter—when I arrived there in June 1977 to begin the summer's work on *Courageous*. I had been in Newport four times, very briefly: once with my parents on a family vacation in 1962; once for a few dawn hours after the 1969 Annapolis–Newport Race;

and for one party in 1974 after the Force 5 North Americans race and again for the start of the 1974 Bermuda Race. I had no idea what to expect as I drove to Rhode Island from the U.S. Merchant Marine Academy at Kings Point, N.Y., where I had been coaching.

Much of what my wife, Janice, and I owned was on the roof of the car. It was late in the evening when we set out, and by the time we crossed the Bay Bridge from Jamestown to Newport the bay was shrouded in fog and it was raining. The view of the bay from the bridge is one of the most magnificent sights on the East Coast, but at 2:00 A.M. we could see nothing other than the road ahead of us, and no sooner had we made the sweeping curve off the bridge into Newport than we were lost. The *Courageous* syndicate had leased Conley Hall, one of the smaller "cottages," for the summer, but I had no idea of how to get there. Early June in Newport is one of the quieter times of the year for the town, and the streets were deserted when a police car came up behind us. Shining a light in my car, the officer asked if he could help us. When I told him that I was with the *Courageous* syndicate and that I was looking for Conley Hall, he said, "Going to spend the summer with us, are you? Follow me." Lights flashing, he escorted us to Conley Hall, a Tudor mansion once owned by a gentleman polo player but now a dormitory of Salve Regina College.

The trees were dripping with fog as we turned into the driveway to the house, which was set back from the street in a grove of trees. The house was silent when I opened the door; those of the crew who had arrived were asleep. I dropped my seabags in the paneled entrance hall, and suddenly the reality of it came to me: We are going to do an America's Cup summer. This is what the sail-testing and the speed trials off Marble-head were all about. Aloud I said to Janice, "This is going to be a good summer. This isn't the junior varsity anymore."

Once *Courageous* won the June trials, the media discovered Turner, and the town, especially on weekends, exploded with visitors, most of whom seemed to view the Cup through the bottom of a beer glass. They drank and we sailed, isolating ourselves from watering holes such as the Black Pearl, whose outside bar on Bowens Wharf was a magnet for would-be sailors and other hangers-on.

Our job was to sail and become familiar with the local waters. What we had to deal with is an area considered one of the nation's great cruising grounds despite its reputation for unkind weather and unpredictable waters. It would be hard to find a body of water that is more cranky than Block Island Sound. With a river (Sakonnet), two bays (Narragansett and Buzzards), Long Island Sound, and the Atlantic Ocean entering into Block Island Sound, there is nothing consistent about it. Fog can roll in from Block Island no matter what the other conditions are; in Block Island Sound you can have wind and fog, no wind and fog, sunshine and fog, and your choice of currents, depending upon the time of the day and the month of the year. This is the area in which we sailed every day in 1977, 1980, and 1983 in a routine that might see us, during the trials, rendezvousing at Brenton Reef Light, a seventy-eight-foot tower mounted on spider-type legs, then heading off in considerable chop to our appointed duels.

Knowing the wind and water patterns was part of my job and I discovered that because of the thermal effect of the land along the coast below Narragansett

Bay you could count on a fairly brisk southwesterly coming up toward the middle of the afternoon. I discovered that there was a big difference in the wind and water conditions the farther away from the Rhode Island shore you were. I learned that when you race in the vicinity of R-2, a red buoy 1½ miles off the beach near the Brenton Reef tower, the right side of the course always is favored. The farther out we went the less land effect we encountered. Out there, the question of whether to sail to the right or to the left was not created by a geographic anomaly or by a thermal or temperature gradient but by wind shifts. Picking the right wind shifts gave us an edge, and by studying the wind and water day after day I was able to make the right decisions as my instincts became sharpened.

The routine was the same every day. Buffet breakfast, then a medium-quick walk to the boat by way of the town's old streets and byways, Turner and I discussing boat and crew problems (not many) and what sails to use or try out that day. In the evening, one was expected to wear tie and blazer to dinner, a tradition established by longtime sailor Lee Loomis, the syndicate manager. After that, if I wasn't going to a movie I'd join Turner in his room to watch his Atlanta Braves play via satellite and talk about the day's practice. Life centered around Conley Hall.

We created our own cloistered community of sailors dedicated to the concept that *Courageous* was indeed a fast all-around boat and was going to win. Go to the boat in the morning, walk with Turner while he picked up trash in the street—loose newspapers, beer cans, and bottles. The effluvia of Newport carousing was anathema to him. "This town is filthy," he would say. "This is my contribution to life in Newport." Go directly back to Conley Hall in the evening for cocktails and dinner. Entertain friends or family at Conley Hall. Life was perfect and paid for—uniforms, laundry, the occasional do given by the New York Yacht Club. Concentrate on the here and now and worry about the rest of one's life in September after the Cup races were all over.

In 1980 we came back to Conley Hall, but Turner was listless and dedicated more to setting up his CNN network than to the fortunes of *Courageous*. Customs had changed, too; blazers and ties were no longer required at cocktail hour or at dinner. A clean polo shirt would do.

In 1982 and 1983 I returned to Newport with the twelve-meter *Defender* to be responsible for. It was hard work trying to solve the mechanical and human problems that went along with that boat. The magic of 1977 had fled; the spirit that Turner had brought to Newport had vanished. Instead we were seeing the beginning of the multidollar, multiboat America's Cup era in which the twelves might as well be constructed out of Japanese rice paper, folded like origami, used for a while, and if unsuitable, thrown away.

Of course there still is magic in Newport today—in the air and on the water—even though the America's Cup scene has switched to Western Australia. On those smoky September afternoons when the moisture in the air filters the sun's rays like tiny prisms and boats are bending to a good breeze out of the southwest, you know deep down, as Hoyt says, that Newport is terminally addictive. You always come back.

*   *   *

ANNAPOLIS:
In a Trance on Spa Creek

Annapolis, Md., is where I live and have made my home since 1977. It is a town of some thirty thousand people, if you count just the little metropolis itself and not the neighboring areas in Anne Arundel County for which it is the county seat. Annapolis is one of the three major sailing centers on the East Coast, and like Newport and Marblehead it shares a bit of early American history and in fact bears a great deal of resemblance to the other two eighteenth-century communities with their historic districts, "antique" houses (as the real-estate brokers now call them), and seagoing quality of life.

Newport has Narragansett Bay and the open sounds leading to the Atlantic Ocean, Marblehead has the ocean and the dimly seen Cape Ann and the northeastern coast, and Annapolis has Chesapeake Bay. The U.S. Coast and Geodetic Survey (now the NOAA) once computed that "the tidal shoreline, detailed, of Chesapeake Bay totals about 5,600 statute miles" against 4,840 miles of the entire United States coastline. We are indebted to Carleton Mitchell, an outstanding writer and yachtsman whose home port is Annapolis, for pointing out that "measurement of each squiggle of each Chesapeake creek to the head of tidewater, or point where the water narrows to the width of one hundred feet, exceeds the coastal outline of the Continental United States." What this really means is that you can cruise Chesapeake Bay practically forever and find a new place to set your hook every night of the cruise. Situated in the central part of the bay's western shore within striking distance of all of these creeks and gunkholes on both sides of the bay, it is no wonder that Annapolis is a haven for Washingtonians, Philadelphians, and Baltimorians who keep their boats in the town's overflowing marinas and themselves in the gentrified houses of the old town, or in new condos on Annapolis's several creeks.

Annapolis was first settled in 1648. Some of its streets still are paved with the cobblestones used as ballast by the sailing ships that called there before the Revolution. It was, for a time, the capital of this country; Congress accepted General Washington's resignation as commander-in-chief of the Continental Army in the state-house in 1783.

Annapolis is an eclectic place, capital of Maryland and site of two major educational institutions, the U.S. Naval Academy and St. John's College, with a very mixed population that includes a professional sailing community of boat designers and builders and a large and very active racing fleet. For me, it seemed an ideal place to make a permanent home when I left the Naval Academy, where I had been the head varsity sailing coach.

Coaching

The U.S. Naval Academy, with forty-one hundred in the brigade of midshipmen, regularly enrolls six hundred in its sailing program, of whom 250 participate in varsity sailing in the dinghies, yawls, and IOR offshore racers. The others are members of the Sailing Club and use the boats recreationally. Without a doubt the Academy has the best-organized varsity sailing program in the nation, there being tacit agreement from the school's administration that sailing builds responsible leaders, which is what the place is all about. Skippers of the IOR racers, with crews of eight to twelve midshipmen or more, are first classmen (seniors), about twenty-two years of age, and they have total responsibility for running their assigned vessels for an entire season, which might include participation during the summer in major national and international regattas. (Each boat also has a "coach," usually an experienced civilian or naval officer who counsels on the operation of the boat but does not command except in emergencies.)

On the New York Maritime varsity we were very much aware of Navy and what their sailors could do; they always were at the top of collegiate regattas, national champions many times. And we envied their facilities: an entire building on the Severn River (the Crown Sailing Center) dedicated to nothing but sailing, with its adjoining large basin and docks for the blue-hulled yawls, the IOR fleet, and the host of one-design dinghies. We envied the Navy sailors, but when it came to running up against the civilian teams, we of the Maritime College and later of the Merchant Marine Academy banded together with the Navy; the military wasn't in favor in the early 1970s, and besides, we all had short hair.

I had been hired by our competitors across Long Island Sound, the U.S. Merchant Marine Academy at Kings Point, as varsity sailing coach—a very prestigious position for a twenty-four-year-old. I worked for the late Captain Joe Prosser, whose emphasis, which I absorbed, was far different from that of the Naval Academy.

Prosser was interested in teaching young people how to do better, not only on the racecourse but also in life. For Joe Prosser, winning was not everything. For instance, I would take the team to the Boston Dinghy Cup for a weekend of racing, return on Sunday evening, and sit down with him on Monday for a cup of tea and a discussion of the regatta.

First he would ask, "Gary, were there any problems? Did anyone get hurt? Did you have enough money?" I would say, "No, Captain, no problems." Then he would ask, "What did you learn over the weekend?" And I would tell him where we had made mistakes, what each of the team members had done in the events, and what they had learned.

Finally he would get around to asking, "Well, Gary, how did you do?" I would say, "We came in third, Captain." And he would say, "I'm glad to hear that, Gary. I'm glad there were no problems."

At the Naval Academy it was different. At the Academy, the emphasis is on goals. For the future officers and gentlemen, winning was everything. If you returned from the Boston Dinghy Cup and had come in third, you got dark looks; it was total disaster as far as the Academy administration was concerned. The emphasis didn't seem to be on getting more of the midshipmen interested in the sailing program but in winning—the same as in all of the school's varsity sports. For the head coaches like myself (dinghies and yawls), the pressure to win was extreme. While it is easy enough to take a small group of sailors and coach them to win, it is much more difficult to achieve this end with a group as large as the Naval Academy's varsity.

My style is different. I believe in guided self-coaching. I watch a race and see mistakes being made. With my experience I clearly see what has gone wrong. But instead of pointing out the mistakes and telling the crew what to do, I ask, "What would you do differently? Did you see what number eight [the winner] did?"

I had learned that each individual should be treated differently from each other; inner clocks and psyches are not the same.

A team member is in a slump and has had three bad races and I say, "Now, calm down and let's drop back and figure out which end of the line is favored." Soothingly I add, "Let's not be the last boat to get on the port tack. Your boathandling is good, but try moving your weight back a little bit."

Another member of the team doesn't react to soothing tones. The only way to make him move is to be strong. "Now, come on! This is ridiculous! You know what you have to do! Now, go out and show 'em!"

One technique that always seems to work is to get the team members to share experiences. Postadolescent athletes tend to be independent, to try to solve their own problems. But you have to get them started by asking Joe Prosser's key question, "What did you learn today?" And "Tell us what happened to you at the leeward mark."

The crews on the offshore boats were interesting. Some of them came to big-boat racing with a great deal of experience; their families usually were involved in sailing, and they might have been on the water since childhood. Others were new at it, but like all of the midshipmen, they were strong and willing and learned fast. For a person like myself, used to the wiles of civilian crews, sailing as a coach with the mids was a pleasure. They are totally disciplined people, used to standing watch and waking up in time, very willing and inner-directed and tough at sea—the ideal mates to be with in an emergency.

Training for offshore racing is not taken lightly at the Academy. Each crew and each boat, under a coach's eyes, has to participate in a flotilla cruise around the Delmarva Peninsula in May before the offshore racing season begins. The course is down Chesapeake Bay from Annapolis, north in the ocean along the coast, up Delaware Bay to the canal connecting the Delaware and the Chesapeake, then down Chesapeake Bay and home.

The cruise is not your average gunkholing expedition but involves serious training in man-overboard procedures, man-aloft, radio techniques, navigation, log-keeping, and watch-standing. Man-overboard drills can occur anytime of the day or night, and the person overboard must be hauled in within a prescribed time, with the coaches keeping score. I consider this training of great importance for future naval officers.

Sometimes the crews get more than they bargained for. On one Delmarva circumnavigation, a fast-moving low-pressure system unloaded a norther on the fleet as it proceeded in late afternoon along the Maryland coast. Within two hours the wind had backed from the southwest to the north, dropping temperatures into the forties, building seas up to fifteen feet. With heavy rain and wind speeds pegged at forty-five knots with occasional gusts as high as sixty, one boat on which an editor served as assistant coach was forced to reduce sail to a small jib and triple-reefed main and without help from a nonfunctioning engine was unable to tack over and turn into Delaware Bay. The crew rode it out despite seasickness and bruises and a sopping-wet interior. At dawn the skies had cleared, the sun illuminating heavy whitecapped seas, and the decision was made to turn tail and sail the boat, a Hood Two-Tonner (about forty feet), into Ocean City, Md. Riding the surf, the vessel was sailed through the narrow dog-legged Ocean City inlet into harbor and docked under sail. At the dock were several other Academy vessels who had made it through the storm with varying degrees of difficulty. But to the observer on board, the ability to take what came and deal with it calmly was impressive.

Cruising

It is not often that a racing man goes cruising. After living in Annapolis for eight years, Janice and I went for a weekend gunkholing trip with friends Eric and Rose Smith aboard their new forty-seven-foot Kaufman-designed sloop.

The rivers and creeks of Maryland's eastern shore offer innumerable places to anchor in the midst of stately trees and three-hundred-year-old estate houses. We elected to sail almost directly across the bay from Annapolis to Shaw Bay, a presumedly peaceful place to drop the hook near Wye Island, where the eastern shore was first settled.

Carleton Mitchell, a racing man who loved to cruise, described a trip he had made through the same waters in these terms:

Bubbles slid along the hull and traced our wake, water furrowed by generations of ghostly ships. Where *Finisterre* now moved, Indians had passed by in crude hollowed logs. Captain John Smith sailed by in 1608 to "perform his discovery." Half a century later, Edward Lloyd of Wye House appeared in the first yacht, "a pleasure boat of 60 tons burthen" complete to "Ensign and pennant with 15 stripes, arms painted thereon, the field azure, the Lion gold . . . and six brass guns fixed on swivels to act in such a manner as to give the greatest report." And here also had passed each development of the age of commercial sail; the Chesapeake log canoe, the pungeye, the ram, the bugeye, even the Baltimore tea clipper, white winged marvel of the world's oceans.

Eric thought that Shaw Bay would be a quiet place to anchor for the first night. "Uncongested" was the word he used. He was far from right; about forty yachts turned up in the harbor for the night. They were generally good neighbors except for the nondescript boat that came through the darkness at about eleven o'clock with the helmsman (male) yelling, "Carol, get the anchor ready!" Everyone in Shaw Bay listened to Carol being harassed by her helmsman. Carol was doing her best, but it took the couple a half hour to find a place to anchor. Then the dissatisfied helmsman made Carol raise the hook and they steamed off for another harbor.

Perhaps the best part of the Kaufman 47 is the way she sails. On Sunday, a solid twelve- to fifteen-knot breeze kicked up and we took the boat to windward for about an hour. The boat is perfect for the bay, drawing just under five feet, with the centerboard up for those shoal areas that border the main channel. With the board down she draws 9½ feet. We passed about forty boats, sailing higher and faster, to the glee of the Smiths. Sailors are like that—competitive even when there is no need to be.

The most enjoyable side of cruising, I discovered, is the time you have for conversation with your friends as opposed to the shouted commands and the constant flow of technical input aboard a racing boat. The ever-changing scene keeps the conversation lively. We found ourselves jibing from Bloody Point on the eastern shore across the bay to Tolley Point on the west and ended up in a discussion about a Freedom 40 that went zipping by downwind, with its sails winged out on either side. Was the boat on port or starboard tack? Finally we decided that the boat, despite its wishbone rig, must be a ketch with the forward mast higher; therefore the forward boom on the port side put the boat on the starboard tack.

Eric had woken up that Sunday morning declaring to the three of us, "Today is going to be the best day of my life." When someone served up the breakfast appetizer of canteloupe, strawberries, and bananas, it was clear that Eric had a point. It was one of the best days of all of our lives, ending in the evening in the town we all called home.

Transcending

Sometimes I like to sail by myself on very small boats such as Sunfish or Lasers. It is a very quiet, concentrated thing to do, especially when there is turmoil all around you. Annapolis has the back creeks and quiet waters for this kind of engagement. Our house backs up on Spa Creek, and one day I took Kristi (2½) out for a ride on the creek in the Sunfish. It was a nice downwind sail of short duration. Then I sat her on the bank with Janice and said, "Watch this, Kristi."

Using the twelve-knot breeze to advantage, I rolled into tack after tack, circled and jibed, spun the boat as if it were part of my body. After a while I was no

longer aware of the shore, of Kristi, of the other boats
in the creek, or of the people who had gathered along
the bank to watch. Somehow I had gone back to my
New York Maritime days when I used to spend afternoons doing a hundred roll tacks around the buoys.
On that day on Spa Creek it was as if I were dancing
on the water, entranced. Only after I realized that the
sound I heard was my neighbors applauding did I come
out of it.

Gary Jobson (standing) started crewing at age six in his Toms River pram.
Photographer A. H. Elmer

Gary Jobson was awarded the Powell Trophy as the Outstanding Junior Sailor on Barnegat Bay in 1966.
Photographer Frank McCain

As *Australia* and *Courageous* met for the first time in 1977, thousands of fans on surrounding ships watched the action. The first windward leg of the America's Cup is really the most important, as the two boats find out exactly what the potential of the other is. *Photographer Dorothy Crossley*

The New York Maritime College sailing team at the 1971 Kennedy Cup. We always had a special rivalry against the Naval Academy, and we enjoyed leaving our uniforms in New York, although our crew looked rather motley. *Photographer U.S. Naval Academy*

Gary Jobson (on right) and Ted Turner (on left, No. 24) first met sailing in the North American Interclass Soling Championships in Barrington, R.I. Jobson used a hiking stick made out of a batten to steer and was able to hike out. *Photographer Ray Medley*

In spite of the great rivalry between *Courageous* and *Australia*, the two crews were good friends before, during, and after the match. After the last race, the two boats returned to Newport Harbor together. *Photographer Betsy Roundsville*

While the press conference following the 1977 America's Cup had a formal air, Ted Turner shows his obvious pleasure at the result.
Photographer Betsy Roundsville

Ted Turner's strong leadership kept the *Courageous* team working together. The daily tow to the racecourse sometimes was as much fun as the sailing itself. Left to right, Bill Jorch (navigator), Robbie Doyle, Gary Jobson, Ted Turner, and Richie Boyd. *Photographer Dorothy Crossley*

Ted Turner
Photographer Gary Jobson

Walter Cronkite
Photographer Gary Jobson

Gary Jobson and Herbert von Karajan
Photographer Dan Wellehan

Conn Findlay
Photographer Christopher Cunningham

George Coumantaros
Photographer Dan Wellehan

Buddy Melges
Photographer Carol Singer

Sam Merrick
Photographer Keith Harvey

Joe Prosser and Janice Jobson
Photographer Gary Jobson

Gary Jobson leads Great Britain in the 1986 Liberty Cup regatta in New York Harbor under the watchful eye of the Statue of Liberty.

CALIFORNIA

I wish they all could be
California girls. . . .

> The Beach Boys

June 10, 1972. The scene is Los Angeles International
Airport. Three of us from New York Maritime College stand by our seabags near an airline baggage car-
ousel. With our short-cut hair, navy blazers, and ties,
we obviously are not Californians. A quick glance in
passing tells you that we are members of some athletic
team, perhaps from the East, although our faces are
windburned and it is clear that we spend a great deal
of time out of doors.

This was our first impression of California—the
crowded airport, the knowledge that we were conspic-
uous, and the sinking feeling that we were in a strange
land. We had come to Southern California to compete
in the Collegiate Nationals, which were being held in
Newport Beach and San Diego. For the three of us (we
were twenty-two), it was our first trip out of the East,
and we didn't know quite what to expect.

I tried not to stare at a long-legged young woman
wearing cutoffs and sandals, a girl who seemed golden
to me with her long blond hair and an undiminished
suntan that covered everything I could see of her. She
took a quick look around to check out the tourists and
then unerringly walked over to us. "Are you Gary Jobson?" she asked. "We're supposed to meet you." Outside, in a blue '68 Mustang convertible, were two more
women who looked just like her, blond and suntanned,

in shorts and polo shirts. Unbelievably, they were playing Beach Boys tapes as we rolled onto the San Diego Freeway and headed south to Newport Beach.

And that's the way it began—twenty-three days of fun, fun, fun, during which we took a third in the sloop Nationals in Newport Harbor and then moved on to Mission Bay in San Diego for the dinghy Collegiates in Flying Juniors. Our California competitors wore Hawaiian-style shirts and stubby shorts and were very brown. They had a strange (to us) way of tacking in which they faced aft as they switched sides—in effect, doing a 360 around the tiller. (This style still is customary in California in dinghy racing as opposed to the technique we used, of passing the tiller from hand to hand behind us as we tacked. This standard method has the advantage of having the helmsman always facing forward.) I took a first in the dinghies, and the team placed second. And we placed third in the district team race. But the week in the sun hadn't ended yet. At the Single-handed Nationals in San Diego, I won ten out of sixteen races in Lasers and took the championship.

Since then I have returned many times to Southern California for the Congressional Cup and other events in Long Beach. And despite the number of years that have gone by since then, I still come as a stranger. I've discovered that the celebrated "laid back" attitude of the locals may be a myth; the yacht clubs are more expensive and formal in their structure and attitudes than the eastern ones. Long Beach is an interesting place to sail, albeit totally tourist-oriented with the *Queen Mary* and Howard Hughes's enormous wooden flying boat, the *Spruce Goose,* on view. At Long Beach, the local sailors know how to play the currents and the thermals; the superheated land initiates a breeze in the afternoon, and they use it to carry themselves to a point offshore just short of where a coastwise current flows.

Californians tend to sail the way they drive: They are boat speed–oriented, not as fond of tacking and covering as Easterners are. The tendency, I have found, is to place more emphasis on straight-line speed and less on tactics, a true philosophical difference. This takes nothing away from the high level of competition and the percentage of Southern Californians who are world-class racers. When San Diego's Gerry Driscoll (Star champion) arrived with *Intrepid* in Newport in 1974 and pushed *Courageous* to the bitter end in the defense trials, the eastern establishment suddenly was faced with the fact that the topflight skippers and crews weren't all from Long Island Sound. Lowell North, Dennis Conner, Dave Ullman, and Tom Blackaller, among others, later proved the point.

Still there is something to be said for heritage. When I am sailing at home and reaching into Annapolis Harbor of an afternoon, with a nice breeze to push me toward the landmark of the statehouse steeple and the brick row houses of the old town gently rippling down the hillside, I often think about that and feel content.

"You'll hit the cliff before you go aground" were the words of veteran ocean racer and tactician Dave Allen while aboard *Jubilation* during the St. Francis Yacht Club's Big Boat Series in San Francisco Bay. The idea was to tack as close to Alcatraz Island as possible to avoid the swift, foul currents between the island and the San Francisco waterfront. Boats ranging from forty to eighty-two feet short-tacked to within a few feet of the island's massive cliffs, only to charge across to the city ferry docks and then short-tack two miles to a windward mark. Thousands crowded the shoreline to get a glimpse of the action as one boat after another spun around the mark, set spinnakers, and flew downwind in twenty- to thirty-knot breezes.

The St. Francis Big Boat Series is one of the nation's premier events for vessels over forty feet and obviously is a showcase for the maxis. During this August week of 1984, seventy-one offshore racers had come to the line, including six giants: *Ondine, Sorcery, Kialoa, Nirvana, Boomerang,* and *Winterhawk. Boomerang* eventually won the event with four firsts and a second, but I came away from the regatta with the mental image of *Nirvana* sailing at eleven knots on a close reach to hit the starting line perfectly while the other five maxis sat near the line, luffing. *Nirvana* popped out into a lead that was not big enough for the newest maxi on the circuit, George Coumantaros's *Boomerang,* to overtake her before the first mark just four miles away.

That is how big boat racing goes in San Francisco Bay, one of the most beautiful natural sailing arenas in the world. It is a testing place for boats and their tacticians, loaded with complicated currents caused by the inflow and outflow of the tide through the Golden Gate. The tacticians keep their own tide books and have their own favorite moves to use, or get out of, the current to keep the boats going on courses that may have ten to twelve legs and be up to thirty-three miles in length through conditions that can change drastically depending upon the section of the bay. Crews are pushed to the limit; many boats sail with four or five extra crew members to use the added weight for ballast on the windward rail. Because of the particularly tricky winds and the suddenness of the gusts, bay racing is noted for some of the most spectacular spinnaker broaches to be seen anywhere.

For me, San Francisco Bay is a yearly mecca. I've sailed in the Big Boat Series five times, raced in six-meter yachts for an entire summer, trained on the twelve-meter *Clipper* there, and participated in a regatta on Australian 18s, probably the most difficult boats in the world to sail well. The ambience is closer to the East Coast than Southern California, and I am more comfortable on San Francisco Bay.

It was on the bay that I had my most embarrassing and potentially dangerous accident in a career that has been remarkably free of them. In 1978, I was recruited by Richard Bertram, noted for his sailing as well as his offshore powerboat racing skills, to sail on *Ondine* in the Big Boat Series. It was my first maxiboat berth, and I wanted to do well. We ended up tying for first in that series (with *Windward Passage*), but almost without me. Carelessly, I had placed my foot into a loop of the mainsheet lying on the deck. We jibed and the mainsheet lifted my foot over my head and I hung there with my left elbow banging into the winches on deck until someone noticed my predicament and let me down.

The next time I sailed in the Big Boat Series was in 1980, after *Courageous* had been eliminated as a defender for the America's Cup. The vessel was *Mistress Quickly,* owned by William Whitehouse-Vaux, and I had been invited by him to skipper the boat, only to discover upon arrival in San Francisco that he had also invited Harold Cudmore and Robby Doyle to do the same thing. The owner's first move was to invite the three of us to dinner, where the check (for four) came to six hundred dollars. We sorted out the afterguard:

Doyle steered, Cudmore was the tactician, and I took on the job of deck boss.

The owner, however, had his mind on other things. "I want to win the regatta," he said. "But the highest priority is the party after the regatta is over."

The affair, for the crew only, was at his house in an exclusive section of San Francisco. There were exotic dancers and a rock band and strange women present and I thought that I had come a long way from the golden girls of 1972.

4

YACHTS

*E*veryone who works has a place where they do it. For some it's an office, for others it may be a laboratory or a workshop or a foundry or their own home. My place of business is a boat—usually one that doesn't belong to me. Over the years of being involved with other people's boats, I've sailed on hundreds of them, but only a few are significant because they represent types of craft that either are influencing the course of sailing or have had an effect on my racing life. In this chapter, therefore, you'll learn about a range of boats that begins with very large catamarans and ends with very small dinghies and includes a look at the twelves and maxis and classic yachts in between.

MEGAMARAN:
That Is Sailing

In the late 1930s or early 1940s, L. Francis Herreshoff wrote a very famous essay called "The Sailing Machine" in which he went to bat for multihulls as the most exciting form of sailing. Said Captain Francis, "The sailor wants to sail [fast] . . . and this reaction can be seen all over the world in the recent interest in catamarans, proas, etc. which can really sail at a good clip and it is my opinion that some sort of sailing machine can be developed which, besides being fast, can be safe, strong and seaworthy."

The concept was not new: Praus, outrigger canoes, and vessels very much like catamarans were the ancient form of travel in the Pacific islands. Nathaniel G. Herreshoff, L. Francis's father, had designed several catamarans, in one of which, according to Captain Nat, ". . . about 1879, I sailed from the west part of Long Island Sound home to Bristol (RI) in one day, a matter of a hundred and twenty-five miles in ten hours."

Concluding his article, L. Francis wrote, "If some future designer can create a craft that will sail a hundred and fifty miles in ten hours, then we can say, 'THAT is sailing.' "

Fleury Michon VII accelerated on every wave. The sensation was like no other I have experienced in sailing. It was as if I were getting on a ski lift, letting the chair spring back and then swing forward with a burst of speed. And this was going hard to weather, not even power-reaching. One of the world's giant "megamarans," *FM VII* is eighty-six feet overall and one of the fastest sailing vessels on the high seas.

I had been invited by her skipper, Phillippe Poupon, to join her on a race from St. Croix in the U.S. Virgin Islands to Martinique, a matter of 366 miles that became a virtual overnighter, even though the distance was sailed, for the most part, upwind.

On *FM VII* all the elements of speed were present, including long waterline, vast sail area, light weight, little wetted surface, and the latest technology in construction, sails, and equipment. The result is power translated into pure speed. Upwind, *FM VII* will do twelve to thirteen knots and tack through a respectable ninety-five degrees. Downwind the boat can do over thirty knots. As she accelerates from wave to wave, the water passing under the hulls appears as if she is riding on a constantly cascading waterfall.

FM VII's statistics are impressive. Forty-five feet separate the two hulls. The mast towers 110 feet off the deck. The boom is forty feet long. With its centerboards down, the boat draws ten feet. The all-up weight, including a crew of seven, is twenty-six thousand pounds—about the same as a forty-seven-foot IOR boat.

FM VII was built of S-glass (a stronger form of fiberglass) and carbon fiber over a honeycomb carbon fiber core. The cost: $450,000, roughly one fourth the cost of an eighty-two-foot IOR maxiracer. The sails are Kevlar. The main has full-length battens from eighteen to forty feet long. The battens alone weigh 140 pounds. The mainsail itself weighs seven hundred pounds.

The two hulls are held together at the bow and stern

by tubular supports. A ten-foot-wide "podium" runs across the middle of the vessel, and that is where the sailing controls are. Halyards and genoa sheets are led to self-tailing winches around the mast. The steering wheels are on either side of the cockpit. A cabinlike housing with a Plexiglas top is installed in front of each wheel. The helmsman stands and steers behind the housing, ducking down as waves and spray smash at the cabin. At these speeds, even tiny droplets of water have the hardness of shotgun pellets.

Just outboard of each steering station are second cabins. On the port side of *FM VII*, the cabin contains a galley, while the navigation area is on the starboard side. There is little headroom, even in a third cabin, which includes a sleeping area consisting of seven-by-seven foot mattress, which three members of the crew share when they are off watch.

The strength of boats like *FM VII* is in their flexibility, but equipment can break. On the delivery from St. Barts to St. Croix for the race start, the centerboard destroyed itself and the No. 2 reef in the main ripped out, leaving the boat to sail with 60 percent of the main. The damage, however, seemed to have little effect on the speed. With the wind blowing twenty knots, not too much time was lost getting to St. Croix.

One disadvantage of the big cats is that they are not easy to maneuver. To tack, one waits for a smooth spot in the waves and then slowly luffs the boat up into the wind. The key is to get the bow just beyond head to wind so that the headsail is backed. Then the bow is forced around on the new course. With the vessel on the new course, the headsail is eased and trimmed in on the new side. The acceleration to full speed takes about fifteen seconds, as opposed to that for a twelve-meter, which won't regain full speed for a minute after the sails are filled. On a twelve a good tack takes about two minutes from the time the helm is put over until the boat regains full speed on its new course.

The sensation of speed on *FM VII* was not like a fast planing dinghy but more like a very powerful freight train that can accelerate very quickly. Most vessels slow down when they hit a wave. *Fleury Michon VII* speeded up. The waterline is so long and the rig so strong (ten different shrouds hold it up) that when the hulls find a flat piece of water, the boat surges forward at an incredible rate. On the wind, the average speed was twelve knots, and when the boat seemed out of control, she was slowed by sailing closer to the wind. At that speed there was very little leeway, although we had difficulty on starboard tack because of the missing centerboard. Reaching, of course, is the best point of sail for the cats. On one reach of several miles, we averaged more than twenty knots with a reduced main and a No. 3 headsail.

Fleury Michon VII had a variety of sails, including a choice of spinnakers. The spinnaker pole is permanently attached to the bow support and looks like the bowsprit on a clipper ship. The spinnaker in the shape of a tube is hoisted aloft inside a cloth cover with the bottom of the cover attached to a bucket. The bucket is hauled aloft and the spinnaker broken out. To douse the sail, the bucket is lowered and pulls the cover over the spinnaker, somewhat like the spinnaker "sally" used on monohull cruising boats.

Skipper Phillippe Poupon's career began in monohulls, first as a dinghy racer in 420s in France. Later he moved to small monohulls, winning many European championships in the class. He had crewed in the

Whitbread Round the World Race but found the lure of the giant multihulls to be the most exciting challenge he could find. In 1984, at twenty-nine, he sailed a sixty-foot predecessor of *FM VII* in the Observer Single-handed Transatlantic Race, taking line honors with a time of sixteen days, twelve hours and was awarded second overall when another vessel was given sixteen hours of time allowance for standing by a disabled craft. Poupon is noted for the way he babies his vessels through storms and squalls. "It does no good to be broken down in the middle of the Atlantic," he said.

When I left Poupon in Martinique, he thanked me graciously for coming on board. "I hope you have had a good time," he said, smiling. "This is the only way to sail."

I left the boat wondering what amazing feats Poupon and *Fleury Michon VII* would be doing next. And in my heart, I knew L. Francis Herreshoff was right. THAT is sailing!

MAXI YACHTS:
Getting Organized

By definition a maxi yacht is an ocean racing vessel that has an IOR handicap rating of sixty feet or higher. A breed of boat is now coming off the drafting tables that ranges about eighty feet overall (the equivalent of IOR's seventy feet) which is what most race organizers around the world have set as the upper size limit. These boats are at the "maximum" size to be entered in any

race that uses the International Offshore Rule for handicapping purposes.

This new breed of boat has an old breed of owners,
men of wealth not unlike the Morgans and Vanderbilts
of yesteryear, who can afford to pick up the check for
a new craft that will come with a base sticker price
(hull only) of about $800,000 to $1 million. After that
the owner turns to an expert to "get the boat organized" with sails, gear, and instrumentation, and his
life becomes an open checkbook: winches, $100,000;
mast and rigging, $90,000; sails, $150,000 (a minimum
of thirty-five sails). There are more thousands to be
spent for designer fees, electronics for navigation and
communication, and for creature comforts (one of the
several transmutations of *Ondine* had a sauna).

Then there is the crew, perhaps twenty-four aboard
one of the major Grand Prix boats. Not everyone can
sail on a maxiboat, but many would like to. We've
mentioned earlier how a successful maxi is a magnet to
that international population of big-boat hands who ship
aboard from race to race or from season to season. But
even among that group, owners and sailing masters pick
and choose experts for each area of the boat. Foredeck
men have to be tall and very strong and quick on their
feet because on the average maxi it takes three men to
handle the spinnaker pole topping lift on a jibe set.
Moving the sails below decks takes four or five persons. Pedestal winches are used for raising halyards and
trimming sheets. Mistakes are costly and dangerous; in
heavy weather, the immense strain on the boat's standing and running rigging is like a time bomb. Blocks
under tension don't break, they explode. During a race,
at least one person in the crew will be bleeding from
some minor injury or other at all times.

You'd better be good; the men who own the maxis are winners onshore and, by God, they are going to win at sea. Here is Jim Kilroy, a California real-estate developer and owner of *Kialoa,* who had a new *Kialoa* built and was hesitant to lose his old one so he used it to speed-test his new yacht. Not many can afford to run two very large yachts at once.

Roger Vaughan, in his book *Fastnet: One Man's Voyage,* provides a glimpse of men like Kilroy to whom big boats may be an extension of power. Vaughan writes:

> The new technology of sailing has given rise to the businesslike, systematized approach to winning as practiced by big businessmen who have become rich enough to enter the game in the first place. Super boats aren't just designed, built and raced; they are organized. Organization is the name of the Super Boat Chess Game. Money, computers and expertise are the pieces. Just like at the office.

If you go one step farther into the superboat syndrome, you discover that while unlimited wealth is a prerequisite for being at the table in this game, there is a difference, as in high-stakes poker, among those who are anteing up. There are yachtsmen. And there are owners.

Yachtsmen may have grown up sailing boats or may have come to it later, working their way from vessel to vessel as their fortunes increased. But they are very committed to their boats, very involved with design decisions and gearing up, and usually they are involved with the sport, too, as members of boards and race committees. They are true skippers, masters of their own vessels. One thinks of Connie van Reischoten, owner and skipper of the great Dutch yacht *Flyer,* winner of the 1983 Whitbread Round the World Race who ran his boat and his crew through the eight-month circumnavigation despite physical problems. Jim Kilroy fits into this category and so does ship broker Huey Long of *Ondine* and shipowner George Coumantaros of *Boomerang* and a handful of others.

As opposed to the yachtsman, the owner pays for the design and boat construction and the gearing up and has the last word on decisions (it's his dollar), but he leaves the organization and the running of the boat and often the sailing of it to others. His boat is the one with the most professionals on it; he counts on them to guide him to the right decisions. Often the boat may race, but he may not be there. When he is there, he probably won't be at the helm; one of the pros will be steering. The owner has his own hidden agenda, including thoughts on why he has gotten into the big-boat game in the first place. One day, if he stays with it long enough, pays attention to his crew, commits himself to the details of his boat, and learns proper regard for the sea, he may become a yachtsman.

Being an owner of a big sailing yacht run by pros, of course, is not a new phenomenon. For more than a century it's the way many wealthy men have gone to sea, and around the turn of the century it spawned a whole group of professional captains, of whom Charley Barr was the most famous. Barr was skipper for J. P. Morgan and August Belmont, among others, raced the America's Cup defender *Columbia* successfully in 1899, and sailed a seventy-foot, one-design sloop called *Mineola* (for Belmont). His most famous exploit was setting a transatlantic record in the German Emperor's Ocean Race from Sandy Hook, N.J., to the Lizard in England in the three-masted schooner *Atlantic*. Barr drove the boat hard, making the crossing in twelve days, four hours.

Barr never owned a boat but always sailed for others, and we are indebted again to L. Francis Herreshoff for accounts of Barr's organizational ability and how he dealt with owners.

According to Herreshoff, Barr told him that it wasn't true (as some had said) that he had driven the owner to his stateroom and kept him there during *Atlantic*'s passage to Europe. Barr's account will sound familiar to anyone who has crewed with an owner on a modern offshore racing yacht:

> One night there came a good beam breeze and I determined to see what the *Atlantic* could do on a reach and when I had everything drawing well, the owner came to me and asked me to shorten sail, to which I said, "Sir, you hired me to try and win this race and that is what I am trying to do." And after we had won the race, he was as pleased as any of us.

If modern maxiracing is a matter of organization, one could learn from Captain Barr, who ran his big commands with crews of Norwegians and Swedes, the vaunted "Scandinavian steam" of those days.

Herreshoff recounted, in *Rudder* magazine:

> He planned a complete day's work for each of the crew, and although all hands were busy all of the time, the yacht at all times was ready to re-

ceive the owner or guests and could have been gotten underway at a moment's notice. All this in great contrast to most yacht captains of that time who only dressed up to go ashore to spend the evening in some gin mill or to boast on some pierhead until the early hours of the morning.

Barr's deck was also a masterpiece of organization:

When he was on one of the larger yachts with first and second mates, quartermasters, etc. he was a strict disciplinarian and after his crew had been trained, the procedure for carrying out an order was about as follows. He had trained his first mate to keep one eye on him, and when Capt. Barr wished to give an order, he simply crooked his forefinger slightly whereupon the mate came close to him. Then Capt. Barr would say very quietly, but distinctly, "Mr. Christiansen, after rounding the next mark I would like the spinnaker set to starboard. I would like the jib topsail replaced with the ballooner."

The mate would then pace slowly up and down the deck watching the marker . . . until he estimated the time and distance right to commence action when he would roar out, "Take in the yib topsail. Raus mit der spinnaker pole to starboard. Stand by for a yibe." Before this moment everything was quiet, the crew of some 20 men all lying prone in a neat row with their heads near the weather waterways. But now, the yacht's deck suddenly changed to a scene of intense activity as each man scrambled to his station and crouched, ready for action.

Getting a modern IOR racing yacht into the water for a new owner is a lesson in organization, tact, politics, patience, and often despair. When the boat is winning, it's fun; when it's not, it's a form of hell. I've been through it once, with *Jubilation*. It's an experience I would think twice about repeating.

Jack James decided to jump into the Grand Prix ocean racing game in 1982 at age fifty. He wasn't entirely new to sailing, having occasionally sailed a catamaran off his Florida home on Useppa Island and also having chartered boats in the Caribbean.

James lived in Tulsa, Oklahoma, where he was the president of Telex Computer Leasing Company and also owned a variety of manufacturing companies as well as a trucking concern. (His parent company eventually became known as Boatman Enterprises, indicating his feelings about yacht racing.)

I first learned of Jack James from George Hazen, a yacht designer and computer wizard in Annapolis who provided computer models of yacht performance and computer-aided design for owners and naval architects. James had been referred to Hazen by way of Bob Bavier, then president of *Yachting* magazine, and the United States Yacht Racing Union. James said he wanted to get into yacht racing and was looking for someone to skipper and organize a new boat. Hazen took on the search project and also sold him a large percentage of his company.

James asked Hazen to contact me, apparently because of my win in the 1982 Hall of Fame regatta. On a trip West that January, I stopped off in Tulsa to see James. Over lunch he asked if I could put together a crew and coordinate the building of a new boat. Somewhat naïve about yacht-racing mores, he suggested that the best way to recruit a crew would be to reward them for doing well; for every first, the skipper would get $1,500, for instance, and the crew, too, would be suitably rewarded. I suggested that the racing organizations would look on this idea with disfavor; ocean racing hadn't quite reached this stage yet.

I suppose that my desire to take a yacht from design through racing led me to agree to his proposal. The first priority was to find a designer. James had the notion he could test the designs of several naval architects in a computer and award the contract to the designer who came up with the fastest boat on disk. He paid $2,500 each to the C&C design group in Canada, California's Nelson/Marek team, Argentina's German Frers and Bruce Farr. The decision was to go with Frers, who had come up with a tried-and-tested hull form; for a new owner, this seemed better than relying on a computer.

Although discussions on building the boat had started in the first week of January 1983, the final decision wasn't made until June, which already put us behind schedule for entering the boat in the SORC in January 1984. There was considerable discussion on whether to build the boat of aluminum or composite glass, but James was ready to try new technology, and the boat was to be built as a vacuum-sealed composite hull by Eric Goetz in Rhode Island. Another month was lost when Goetz ran behind schedule in clearing the decks with construction of the Sparkman & Stephens-designed *Golden Eagle,* a fifty-two-footer.

In the meantime, James and his wife, Carol, moved from Tulsa to Montecito, Calif., taking possession of several acres of land and a luxurious house with a view of the hills around Santa Barbara and the Pacific beyond. Under Carol's direction decorators made a showpiece out of the place, not forgetting to install a glass case for all the trophies the boat, yet unnamed, would win.

Finding a suitable name took some time; many were considered, including *Speed Rack,* the name of one of his companies. James was informed that Rule 26 of the yacht racing rules prohibits advertising on the hull sides, and Carol came up with the name *Jubilation.*

At about that time, George Varga, a *Tenacious* veteran and captain on Al van Metre's famed *Running Tide,* was hired as captain, the first of the crew to sign on. Varga's task was to oversee the boat construction, staying with the vessel, in effect, from birth on.

Jubilation's start was not the most propitious. First, during sea trials, she ran aground while being motored up the Barrington River, damaging her keel. Then, at the launching, with ice in the river, it took three tries for Carol James to break a bottle of champagne across the bow.

This was January 7, 1984, with the first SORC race thirty days away and the boat needing to be trucked to Florida and test-sailed. Two more disappointments intervened. The sail manufacturer had put together a $105,000 sail inventory, but while some of the sails were good, others did not match up to James's expectations. We also had major problems with the mast. The mast section promised by the manufacturer was not available, and a heavier section was substituted that never performed well, besides being too heavy for a mast of its size. (The following September we replaced the mast with a spar that was 130 pounds lighter and the boat performed much better.)

Still, despite all of the problems and the addition of an ill-advised twenty-eight hundred pounds of ballast in front of the mast, *Jubilation* finished a respectable fifth at the SORC. In Chesapeake Bay that spring, the boat began to pick up trophies. Racing on Long Island Sound during the summer, the boat captain, at the helm, got involved in a major collision to the tune of $1,500 worth of damage to the other vessel. Then later in the spring came the Onion Patch Series off Newport, and *Jubilation,* with the twenty-eight hundred pounds of misplaced lead removed, woke up and placed second in all three races. In the Bermuda Race, following the Onion, *Jubilation* had one of her finest hours, placing second of nineteen in Class A and fourth in fleet as she succeeded in locating the helpful Gulf Stream meander. James was a happy man when we arrived in Hamilton and saw the placings on the TV screens in the Royal Bermuda Yacht Squadron.

But near the top of the fleet was the closest *Jubilation* would ever come to winning. The lesson I learned is that when you go for a good, all-around boat, that is exactly what you get. If we sailed *Jubilation* with a top crew, ran a perfect start, and hit every wind shift correctly, we would sometimes just barely win, but most often we would end up second or third, and this is the way it turned out during the remainder of my tenure as skipper of the boat at SORC, Antigua Race Week, Block Island, and Cowes.

For me, it was all over but the traveling. James, now a member of the St. Francis Yacht Club, had decided to ship the boat from Cowes to San Francisco for the 1985 Big Boat Series. It was a ten-thousand-mile odyssey rarely equaled in our time. Remember, *Jubilation* is fifty-four feet long; fifteen feet, six inches wide; stands fifteen feet from the bottom of the keel to the top of the deck; weighs forty thousand pounds; and is accompanied by an eighty-foot mast. Here are some notes from my log:

August 14: Jubilation is disassembled by crew. Winches, pulpits, and lifelines are stowed below. All sails are dried and packed. Mast is pulled, boat is hauled at Plymouth.

August 15: Truck sets off with boat but thirty miles out of Plymouth is stopped by British authorities, who pronounce the truck unsafe for further travel. Driver spends two days arranging for another truck without telling *Jubilation*'s owner or her professional captain.

August 18: Sealand ship in Felixstow waits ten hours past scheduled departure time for *Jubilation*'s arrival. Driver, truck, and yacht are missing. *Jubilation* arrives six hours after the ship leaves.

August 20: Legal action initiated against the British trucking company.

August 21: A second ship due to depart from Felixstow for Fort Lauderdale, Fla., agrees to take *Jubilation*.

August 23: Jubilation departs aboard ship.

August 30: Ship encounters Hurricane Elena. Puts in at Savannah, Ga.

September 3: Jubilation arrives in Fort Lauderdale. Joelle Trucking, hired to haul *Jubilation* to San Francisco, has not arrived.

September 4: Joelle Trucking arrives, but steamship company and dock crew refuse to move boat until all paperwork has been cleared.

September 6: Jubilation loaded on truck. Miami authorities refuse a permit to travel through the city because of weekend traffic.

September 9: Jubilation leaves Miami, en route to California.

September 13: Jubilation, on tractor-trailer with accompanying escort vehicle, crosses Nevada/California line at 1:30 P.M. California Transport Authority promptly orders truck, trailer, and yacht to be completely inspected, but not until Monday morning, September 16.

September 15: First race of Big Boat Series. *Jubilation* is on the state border awaiting a permit to proceed.

September 16: Truck is authorized to proceed on secondary roads only to Vallejo, via Sacramento. Second of five races is completed in San Francisco Bay.

September 17: Lay day for Big Boat Series. At 12:30 P.M., *Jubilation* arrives at ABC Yacht Yard in Vallejo, where the crew begins assembling the boat to prepare it for racing at 1:00 P.M. the following day. The rest of the day goes like this:

3:00 P.M.: Funds cleared and *Jubilation* off-loaded.

4:00 P.M.: High tide. Boat must be launched within two hours.

4:30 P.M.: Crane company cancels, mast cannot be stepped.

5:00 P.M.: Second crane company is bribed to step mast.

5:30 P.M.: Crane arrives.

6:00 P.M.: Boat launched, but tide is too low now. Boat must be wedged into the water by sixteen people using four-by-four planks.

6:30 P.M.: Boat cleared from hoist and mast installed.

7:00 P.M.: *Jubilation's* engine will not start. Towboat hired to tow *Jubilation* into channel.

7:15 P.M.: Engine starts. *Jubilation* motors through mud into deep water.

8:00 P.M.: Boat motors forty miles to St. Francis Yacht Club, arriving at 11:30 P.M.

September 18: *Jubilation* places fifth out of twelve in Class B.

September 19: *Jubilation* is hauled to have bottom cleaned and have remaining equipment installed.

September 20: *Jubilation* takes another fifth place.

September 21: Jubilation places seventh in the final race of the Big Boat Series.

That ended my association with the owner and with *Jubilation*. After a respite of six months James hired a new skipper and mostly new crew. I have not really heard from him since, although one postscript was reported to me much later.

James contracted with yacht designers John Reichel and Jim Pugh to go over the boat thoroughly and check its measurements for the IOR. All IOR vessels have "bumps" on the hull where the measurements are taken. Jim Pugh found that the builder had not placed the measurement bumps correctly—that two of the three bumps were six to seven inches off, and the third was two to three inches off, in effect penalizing *Jubilation* unfairly in her handicap rating. It also was found that her keel was out of shape, and a new elliptical keel was cast and set in place.

The boat is going much better these days. In fact, in June 1986, *Jubilation* won Long Beach Race Week. Although I am no longer part of the crew, I was happy that James had finally attained his goal.

DINGHIES:
Roll Tack, Roll

Recently I have been sailing dinghies again. After years of big-boat racing, my favorite form of competition now is in small boats. It's not nostalgia for my high-school and college racing days that is getting me out on the waters around Annapolis on those brisk fall weekends, but small voyages of rediscovery. I am re-learning how fine it is to be one with the boat, to control the craft with weight, sail trim, and tiller. In big boats, it's boat speed. In the one-design fleets, sailing is a tactical and boathandling game, a struggle of strategies and cleverness on a handkerchief of a course.

I've raced many boats in the dinghy line—Sneakboxes, Penguins, Interclubs, Tech dinghies, International 10s and 12s, 420s, 470s, Flying Dutchman, Finns, Lasers, even a Sunfish or two—a tiny percentage of the one-design boats available in this country. In the Annapolis area, the dinghy of choice is the Snipe, a rather simple little boat that is giving the lie to the rumor that one-design racing is dying a slow death. Ten new Snipes are joining our little fleet at the Severn Sailing Association. The growth is taking place elsewhere, too; in Marblehead, Mass., for many years a hotbed of dinghy racing, Snipes are taking the place of classes that are slowly fading into the horizon, such as International One-Designs (IODs) and US-1s.

Snipes have been around for years. Essentially a two-man dinghy, the boat is 15½ feet long with a sloop rig and carries no spinnaker. Designed by *Rudder* editor and naval architect William Crosby, building plans for the boat, as was the custom, were available through the magazine. The first Snipe appeared in 1931 on the western coast of Florida, and an article about the boat turned up in the July issue of *Rudder* that year. As *Rudder*'s policy was to name all of its boat-plan vessels after seabirds, Crosby called his new design a Snipe, and the name has stuck for more than half a century. To Crosby's surprise, the July issue was sold out; orders for boat plans came flooding in, and his dinghy was a success.

One can see why. The Snipe is simple and inexpensive to build (Crosby, in 1931, figured you could build one for $100) and easy to maintain. Even in today's terms, a Snipe is cheap. For less than $5,000 one can have the top-of-the-line boat in fiberglass, all of the deluxe fittings and equipment, an extra mast, two jibs, a trailer, and top and bottom covers.

Today there are more than twenty-five thousand Snipes throughout the world, with perhaps more than five hundred fleets in thirty countries. McClaughlin & Company builds them at the rate of two a week in a plant in Tennessee. But they are built overseas as well; a Danish Snipe is imported into the United States. The key to any one-design's success is strict control of the boat's fabrication and its allowable gear, and promotion of the class through communication among its members. Snipe sailors are enthusiasts; they travel outside their own regions for regattas and are involved with junior training to keep the class going. They are not enthusiastic about the boat ever becoming an Olympic class, feeling that such a move would encourage building techniques and the laying on of expensive go-fast gear that would take the boat away from the average sailors who enjoy it now and put it into the hands of the experts.

Experienced sailors like the Snipe because of its tactical challenges; it is not a boat-speed freak's yacht. It seems easy to be competitive in a Snipe, and even older boats do well. In fact, I was so convinced that I bought one.

There is a camaraderie among adult dinghy sailors that I missed during the hotly competitive racing days of my youth. On the course it's as tough to win as ever. One Saturday eighteen Snipes showed up for the regatta. There were nine races, and no one won more than one race. We've introduced match racing (one on one), which has become popular because sailors find their own level and eventually race other entrants at that level. Somewhat more sophisticated is team racing (three on three), where the object is not necessarily for everyone on the team to place high but to protect your would-be winner by tactically holding off the other guys.

The spicy days of racing in fall and winter end in the early darkness. The boats are lifted out of the water, put on their trailers, and washed down. In the evening we repair to someone's house for beers and an old-fashioned covered-dish buffet. Often when I've been traveling, leapfrogging from airport to airport and going aboard one big boat after another, I think about the charm of racing little boats on the Severn.

One of the great pleasures of dinghy racing is that doing it well takes all your body. Even on the Snipes, I still practice roll tacking, which for a dinghy racer has the joy of a skier doing perfect parallel turns on a steep ski slope. Earlier I mentioned spending hours every afternoon practicing roll tacks around the pilings at New York Maritime; recently I've been doing it as an exercise in small-boat control and as a way to retain a feel for dinghy sailing.

The art of roll tacking is in the coordination of your weight, sail trim, and rudder at the same time. You have to go from one side of the boat to the other and maintain the exact angle of heel. You start by deciding to tack, looking for a puff of wind and a smooth spot in the water. Put the helm across slowly, simultaneously pulling in the sail and leaning to windward. When the mainsail luffs and you are head to wind, push the helm over faster and scoot your body from one side to the other. I do it best by taking my legs out of the hiking straps before beginning the tack. When one toe hits the bottom of the boat I instantly go out on the strap on the other side, ease the sail, heel over, and then rock the boat back to accelerate for speed.

Roll tacks. They're in my blood. And in my dreams.

SCOWS, E THROUGH M:
They Got Me Traveling

On Barnegat Bay, that shallow body of water on which I spent many hours trying to become a sailor, you could have your Sneakboxes and your Penguins, but the classy boat to race was the scow. I suppose that the boat's prestige came from the fact that Barnegat Bay was the only place that scows were raced outside the Midwest, where they were born. The bay perfectly suited their temperament; the water was mostly shallow, the winds could pipe up, but unless there was a major storm, the seas were reasonably flat. It was perfect territory for the scows, which look like giant surfboards with cock-pits; they have no underbody to get you in trouble on the shoals. The scows skittered across the water like skipping stones. They were not easy to sail. Without a ballast keel, they were held down by two relatively short bilge keels that were unballasted but were intended to give the boat stability. They sailed best on a heel; to an observer they seemed just on the edge of capsizing, and their stability was aided by the crew practically stand-ing on the windward hullside.

In short, sailing a scow was what the men did, and if any of them deigned to ask if you could "help out next weekend," it was like being touched by the hand of God. Racing on a scow put you in the land of adults; the boats were too tough for kids, and getting on one

was a rite of passage on Barnegat Bay. Four made up
a crew, and when Sam Merrick, considered one of the
best sailors on the bay, asked me if I could "help him
out" aboard his E-scow in weekend racing, I leaped at
the chance.

Sam, who headed the successful American Olympic
sailing effort in 1984, was my mentor in the 1960s and
during those seven years of sailing with him developed
the idea of feeding a skipper tactical input. I found myself making recommendations, and instead of saying,
"Shut up, don't talk to me," as other skippers had, he
appreciated the flow of words about what was happening around us during the regatta so that he could concentrate on steering. His pride went into sailing the boat
well along with winning; the 28-foot E-scows were
aesthetically beautiful, with their fractional rigs and raked
masts. But strangely enough they sailed fastest not when
they were flat, but on their ears. When they were heeled
over, it took strength to get on the windward rail and
hike out. And because of their phenomenal speeds (over
twenty knots), decision-making had to be instinctive.
There was no time for mistakes.

Scows were a product of some fertile minds at the
Inland Lake Yachting Association of Milwaukee, Wis.,
who were looking for a one-design boat to be raced on
midwestern lakes and that would supplant the mess of
catboats and small sloops that were trying to race but
without much organization. Sometime before the ILYA
was established in 1898, one of its future members, Lu-
cius Ordway, Sr., knowing of Nathanael Herreshoff's
interest in flat-bottomed hulls, had a twenty-footer
(*Mahta*) designed that was called a scow but that lacked
the convention that all true scows have—ribs across the
bottom, like a canoe. The first scow regatta, with a
small entry list, was held on White Bear Lake, Mich.,

with *Mahta* winning the twenty-foot class. The first true scow, a vessel designed by New York naval architect Charles A. Reed, was built at White Bear Lake shortly thereafter. Very quickly scows began appearing on midwestern lakes, under the control of the ILYA, which established one-design rules for the boats. At first, there was a whole alphabet of scows—A boats at 38 feet, B-scows at thirty-two feet, C-scows at twenty feet. In 1924, the E-scow replaced the B and has been with us ever since. Today we have the M-scow (M-16), at sixteen feet, to add to the list.

To Easterners, weaned on traditional one-design hulls or bigger conventional sloops, the scows seemed like a joke. With their long, narrow hulls, duckbill bows, and flush decks, there was something freaky about them as they moved over the water, not through it. But when they saw what an A-scow could do—twenty-five knots on a power reach, setting a thousand feet of sail—they became believers. And when skippers like Buddy Melges who had been trained on scows began winning national regattas, they became complete converts.

Sam Merrick and his E-scow *Windquest* were home to me. I crewed in every position on that boat, including skipper, tactician and mainsheet trimmer. It was an education that got me traveling.

CLASSIC YACHTS:
More Than One Life

For years, all the major offshore racing boats I've sailed have been state-of-the-art vessels, miracles of modern yacht-building with their lightweight aluminum or composite hulls, miracle-fabric sails, and electronic navigation and instrumentation systems. State-of-the art, however, doesn't necessarily translate into comfort at sea or the ability to go for days without destroying the crew. Motion-caused fatigue is an overwhelming factor in modern racing yachts. Crew quarters always are cramped or virtually nonexistent, sail stowage sometimes being more important than space for men. Galleys can be minimal, all in the interest of saving weight. The vessels are like trinkets on the sea, all parts of the boat working violently as it charges through the water. At speed, sailing on a Grand Prix racer, even one of the maxis such as *Condor,* is like being aboard an enormous, fast-moving cork.

To understand how difficult modern yacht racing really is, one has to sail aboard one of the classic yachts still at sea. These greyhounds were built for comfort as well as speed. It was assumed by their designers that the ability to go fast and win long-distance ocean races need not compromise the below-decks accommodations. Their owners and skippers lived well. There was a sufficiency of heads, the galley (sometimes with a coal stove) was meant to feed the crew well, and each crew member had his own berth, as opposed to the shared flimsy pipe and canvas arrangements on some modern yachts.

On deck, they showed the shipwright's art, with teakwork and carved rails, and scarfing that was practically invisible. The desire to make the boat aesthetically perfect was not meant to interfere with their primary purpose, speed over long distances. In the years before World War II, races to Europe were the norm rather than the exception, and the boats that survived

continued the tradition after the war in such events as
Marblehead–Halifax and Newport–Bermuda and several races to Scandinavia.

Ticonderoga, the famed L. Francis Herreshoff-
designed clipper-bowed ketch, was unbeatable for many
years in distance racing. Seventy-two feet overall, she
could set twenty-eight hundred square feet of sail.
Among the exquisite hand carvings on the boat were a
pair of gold-painted dolphins on the beam rails; to "bury
the dolphins" was a sign that the big *Ti* was at her
best, as she would be moving along at over twelve
knots. Below she had a huge open saloon, a separate
galley, and berths for twelve people to sleep in comfort.

These boats do not fade away easily. They have many
lives. *Royono,* on which I sailed and learned to appre-
ciate the power of the classic yachts, had many transmutations. A famous Alden design, she was christened
Mandoo II when she was launched in 1936 as a masthead yawl, and she raced as a cutter in the 1938 Bermuda Race.

A description of her in Carrick and Henderson's *John
G. Alden and His Yacht Designs* shows what she was
like then (not much different from when I sailed on her):

> The yawl is essentially a flushdecker, but the
> sweep of the decks is interrupted by two small cabin
> trunks, several skylights and a booby hatch for-
> ward. The owner has a large stateroom with a pri-
> vate head aft and there is a guest stateroom
> immediately forward, off the so-called lobby. Op-
> posite that and convenient to the companionway
> ladder are another enclosed head and a chart table.
> The galley and captain's cabin opposite are just
> forward of the comfortable saloon. As one would

expect, there are bunks and a head forward for the professional crew.

Later, *Mandoo II* was sold to a midwestern owner, John B. Ford, who changed her name to *Royono* and raced her successfully on the Great Lakes. In 1950 she was donated to the U.S. Naval Academy and competed in two successive Bermuda races, placing third in class in 1950 and first in class in 1952. The story of *Royono,* however, hadn't ended. For a while she was in Miami, operated as a charter vessel, then fell into the hands of drug smugglers who gutted her to carry loads of marijuana. When the smugglers fell into the hands of the Coast Guard in 1973, the vessel was impounded in Florida and finally sold at auction for $25,000. Her new owners rebuilt *Royono* at considerable expense and put her into the Caribbean charter trade, where she is now.

You can see and visit many of these boats at the Classic Yacht Regatta held late every summer in Newport, R.I., where the boats not only race but also are shown off by their proud crews and owners. The mahogany rails gleam to perfection, the teak decks are sanded white and varnished with a dozen coats. Rafted up on the outside docks, they transport you into another time when beauty was as important as "a fair turn of speed."

One year I sailed *Formidable,* an old but very capable M-boat, in the Classic Regatta. She was eighty-four feet long and not happy with the light air; she wanted a breeze to get her going. But when I stood behind the wheel I knew I had something underfoot that would never die.

THE TWELVES

The America's Cup is really
just a game of life and we
use the twelve-meters to keep score.

Dennis Conner

The memory of what it was like first to sail on a twelve-meter yacht takes me back to a hill in Marblehead in the spring of 1977. It had been a day of baptism aboard *Courageous,* trying to learn something about sailing a twelve and also how to work with Ted Turner, who had signed me on as tactician. That evening I stood with Turner on Old Burial Hill, Marblehead's three-hundred-year-old parklike burial ground that is one of the highest points in the town. It is a quiet place, with old gravestones set among the rock ledges and a monument to the sixty-five men and boys of the Marble-head fishing fleet who died at sea in a sudden northeast storm in 1846, leaving forty-three widows and 155 children to survive as best they could.

On Old Burial Hill, a sailor can come to terms with himself and his connection with the sea, and even Turner was silent as we looked far below at Little Harbor, where *Courageous* and *Independence* were docked. The winches gleamed, the decks had been freshly washed, and members of the crews could be seen in their new uniforms.

Finally Turner looked at me and said, "When you were fifteen years old, did you ever think you would be sailing on boats like these?" I thought for a minute, surprised to hear Turner, who was so successful in business and ocean racing, ask a question like that. "No," I replied. Turner followed, "Well, neither did I. Isn't it the greatest thing that has ever happened?"

And for both of us it was, because back then only a handful of sailors had the opportunity to race on twelve-meter yachts. In 1977 there were six twelves vying to be in the America's Cup. As the crew on a twelve is limited to eleven, there were sixty-six sailors aboard the yachts when they came together in Newport. In 1980, there were eight twelve-meter yachts sailing in the world (eighty-eight in crew); three years later, in 1983, the number had almost doubled, to fifteen yachts (165 in crew). In 1987, with the America's Cup turned into less of a regatta and more of an industry, there are forty-four twelves, thirty-one of which are brand-new, crewed and supported by what seem to be a cast of thousands—484 sailors plus uncounted handlers.

What is even more remarkable is that in 1974, when *Courageous* was launched in the midst of a fuel crisis and when irate Americans were questioning the relative priorities of spending $1.5 million on what appeared to be a game of toys for the rich, there was much talk about the death of the twelves. In fact, one *Courageous* syndicate member, a Philadelphia lady who had been an ardent backer of the New York Yacht Club boats, pulled out her support, suggesting that there was something improper about having an America's Cup and all of the Newport social events connected with it when the country was in crisis.

A typical boating magazine article was headed, "Is This the Last Summer of the Twelves?" Peter Swerdloff, in *Rudder* magazine (May 1974), wrote:

> Twelve Meters are beautiful boats. Even with their noses clipped, à la *Intrepid,* and their tran-

soms reversed, they are long and graceful, tall and powerful and fast. But beautiful as they are, even more than in the past, many boatmen are wondering if the time, money and talent that is poured into America's Cup competitors could be better lavished on some other type of yacht. Twelve-Meter sloops, it is felt, are going the way of the J-boats.

The writer then goes on to express the still-held view that the America's Cup is anachronistic, "that it retains its special place in history precisely because it is hopelessly old-fashioned, frightfully costly and utterly useless."
Despite these cries of doom, twelve years later, as anachronistic as it might be, the America's Cup goes on, with no end in sight, sailed in boats designed to a measurement rule that is eighty years old. How to explain it?
It may be that western Australian businessman Alan Bond's determination to get himself a winner after three successive losses in Newport had something to do with it. *Intrepid*'s split-rudder hull had been the bench mark for twelve-meter design for so many years that the Americans were comfortable with it; all of the twelve-meter yachts designed on this side of the world were versions of the *Intrepid* hull form. So were the Australian vessels until after 1980, when Bond, defeated again, decided along with his naval architect, Ben Lexcen, that twelve-meter design was in a box and that the only way to wrest the Cup from its ancestral perch at the New York Yacht Club was to break out of the box with something radical but workable. Lexcen's solution was the winged keel imposed on Bond's 1983 challenger, *Australia II,* which combined with a hard-

working, psychologically up crew went on to make history.

Perhaps it's the challenge of this technological breakthrough showing that some freedom of design still exists under the Twelve-Meter Rule that has brought the onslaught of new twelves to Fremantle, Australia, to compete in the 1987 regatta. Bond proved that it is possible to attain what seemed unattainable to take the America's Cup away from the New York Yacht Club. Yacht clubs and syndicates of six nations are trying to prove that he may be right.

Or is the competition inspired by the glory of such classic-looking vessels match-racing *mano-a-mano*? There is nothing more beautiful on the sea than two twelves circling at the start, sails taut, crews searching for the break that will take them over the line first at the gun. Their sails are sculptured; their decks clean of lifelines and any clutter so it is easy to see the elegant curve of their sheers; the forestay makes one continuous taut line to the masthead. They are living exponents of geometric forms on the sea.

Yet the Twelve-Meter Rule is their undoing. It is a complicated formula in which certain set factors of measurement must equal twelve. Within the formula lie the loopholes that yacht designers have been exploiting for years. But one principle of the formula is very clear: Whatever is added in one area must be taken away in another to avoid being penalized. For instance, a twelve-meter cannot be narrower than 3.6 meters (11.8 feet) without penalty. The maximum height of the sailplan cannot be more than 25.18 meters (82.6 feet) above the covering board. Total sail area for the average twelve is about 167 square meters (eighteen hundred square feet). There is a formula for minimum displacement that comes out on the average twelve to about sixty thousand pounds. Twelves can be anywhere from sixty-three to sixty-seven feet overall, with a waterline length of about forty-four to forty-eight feet.

The anachronism is in what this formula produces when the twelves take to the water. They are long and heavy and not easily maneuvered (*Defender* weighed fifty-six thousand pounds; a comparative IOR ocean racer would weigh forty-two thousand pounds). Even *Australia II,* which surprised her American opponents with the maneuverability provided her by winged keel, took great teamwork aboard to keep her viable. Twelves point extremely high, but they are slow to accelerate after a tack. They are undermanned; the Twelve-Meter Rule calls for a maximum of eleven in crew compared to a sixty-five-foot ocean racer, which probably would have fourteen. A twelve, of course, is a huge day racer and doesn't sail distance or night races, but the eleven crew members still have to know what they are about. They have to be well-rounded, equally adept at sailing upwind, downwind, reaching, running, and tacking.

In 1983, we invited *Sail* Associate Editor Robby Robinson, a twelve-meter veteran and experienced sailor himself aboard *Defender,* to give the magazine's readers some idea of what it takes to maneuver a twelve. "Tacking is so important," he wrote, "because it happens so often—an average of more than 30 times in a full course (24.6-mile race). A half-second edge per tack in getting back to course and speed can therefore spell a 15-second (three-boat-length) advantage in a normal race. That's a big edge."

"The theory is simple," I told Robinson as we sailed out. "Because the boats are so heavy and difficult to get started, keeping the speed up is the big thing. Rudder action slows the boat down, so we trim the main to help in bringing the boat into the wind. There is a school of thought that says you should hold onto the jib and let it back to help the bow move farther around. Backing slows you down, though. We try for the least amount of backing, just enough to get the jib through the foretriangle. Sometimes the jib seems to take days to slide by the mast. To accelerate as quickly as possible on the new tack, you power up both the main and jib. As the speed builds you trim and adjust until you are back to course and speed."

Robinson's portrayal of how we tacked *Defender* is the most accurate description of this maneuver aboard a twelve that has ever been published, in my estimation. It provides a true picture of the absolute teamwork demanded of a twelve-meter crew:

The breeze is 18 knots over the deck, the swell from the south is regular and we are within 23 or 24 degrees of the apparent wind as we cream along closehauled on starboard tack. The 11 crewmen in racing positions move very little. The bowman and three of the four grinders are hiked along the starboard rail, prone with one arm and a leg draped outboard. Inboard are the tailers (in their foxholes) and the port after-grinder. The mainsheet man is aft, to weather of his center console. Next come the tactician (to starboard) and the navigator (to port) and finally the helmsman (braced and standing behind the weather wheel).

"Starting a slow tack in three boat lengths," says the tactician. No one signs or moves. "One." The grinder turns his handles at three-quarter speed. The port tailer trims an inch of jibsheet. "Starting a slow tack . . . Now!"

With hands crossed to work both the trim tab (inner rim) and rudder, the skipper begins his tack. "Seven point eight," calls the navigator, giving the speed. He punches his watch and takes slack out of the leeward running backstay. The mainsheet man horses the traveler to weather, the bowman and the winch grinders come in from the rail. The skipper eyes the waves to weather and continues to double-steer. "Seven point six."

For a frozen instant, her sails still full, her crew all poised, the Twelve carves her way to weather in relative silence. The wave whoosh lessens, she straightens slightly, she slows imperceptibly. "Seven point five." The jib scallops and refills. No sound, little motion. The jib begins its second break. Coils fly from the drum in front of the leeward tailer. The boat bolts near upright with surprising snappiness. A flurry erupts of clanging wire on shrouds, clacking vang car in its track, and cracking thwopping Kevlar/Mylar in three-quarter time. Bowman and starboard tailer take in overhand bights of tacking line and jibsheet respectively. The genoa, pleated by the tacking line, hangs poised to pass through the foretriangle. Navigator and tactician work their respective running backstays; the mainsheet man tweaks and trims, the skipper takes a cross step beneath the boom to the port wheel. The upright boat spins sedately to starboard. "Seven point zero."

The genoa clew clears the mast, the bowman casts off the tacking line, the starboard tailer yells, "Go!" and grinder handles fly. Linked to the starboard drum, four big men pour enough power into the system to overcome thousands of pounds of

The reason the *Courageous* crew did so well is we all helped each other out. No one was ever excused from wet-sanding the bottom. *Photographer John Mecray*

Jubilation leads *Check Mate* in a tight race on San Francisco Bay in the 1984 Big Boat Series. *Photographer Sharon Green*

After winning the America's Cup, the crew throws each other in. For me this was one of the highlights of my life. *Photographer Christopher Cunningham*

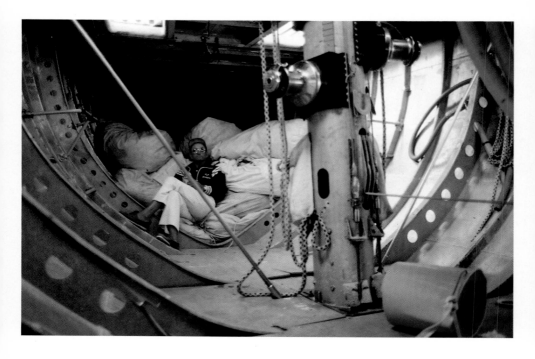

Marty O'Meara belowdecks on *Courageous* pressing sails, with a twelve-meter head seen in the lower right. *Photographer Christopher Cunningham*

s was the closest that *Courageous* and *Australia* ever got during the 1977
erica's Cup. *Photographer Daniel Forster*

Jubilation got off to a fast start in the 1985 SORC by crossing the fleet on port tack at the start. *Photographer Sharon Green*

The Royal Perth Yacht Club attracted fourteen twelve-meters to race togethe
the 1986 World Championship. It is a shame that the twelve-meters never rac
as a fleet in Newport, R.I. *Photographer Daniel Forster*

load and make the wire fly off the drum in a blur. The load increases, the boat leans to starboard, the flogging and clanging stops. The well-oiled growl of the big winch is the dominant sound. "Shift," says the starboard after-grinder and the handles turn fast the opposite way while the wire slows to half speed. "Six point eight."

"Back," comes the call from the same grinder. Pumping more easily, the four men reverse direction again and bring in the last foot of sheet to an "easy, easy, easy . . . good" from the starboard tailer. The helmsman resets the trim tab; the mainsheet man continues shaping; the bowman eases the jib halyard. "Six point six." This part of the spin has taken 11 seconds.

The Twelve shoulders into the new tack and heels more now than she will at speed. The wave sounds and the squeaks of the mainsheet man's magistry are background for the tailer's calls. "Half up on the halyard. Make it twenty-five hundred pounds on the runner. Bow down three degrees."

"Six point four," says the navigator.

Using cunningham, outhaul, mast ram and permanent backstay as well as sheet and traveler, the mainsheet man continues singlehandedly to massage the shape of the big sail. Manipulating halyard tension, headstay sag (via tension on the running backstay—worked by the navigator and tactician) and a wide range of lead positions, the tailer suits the jib to the wind angle and speed. Occasionally he calls for a change in course: "Six point four" . . . "Bow down two degrees" . . . "Six point six" . . . "Seven point zero" . . . "Seven point two" . . . "Bow up two de-

grees" . . . "Seven point four" . . . "Seven point
six . . . speed!" The Twelve is back to speed on
her close-hauled course. The slow tack has taken
64 seconds.

Robinson captured how complex, demanding, and
beautifully synchronized this single tack was, and it was
only one of several thousand tacks we did that summer. Between this relatively uncomplicated maneuver
and more complicated evolutions that the crew must
do perfectly, like jibe sets, life aboard a twelve is very
unglamorous and physically and mentally wearing.

The routine for the crew is the same every day. Exercise in the morning. Go to the boat and perform
maintenance chores. Go out and practice or race with
the same persons you have been with for more weeks
than you care to think about. Bring the boat back to
the dock and put it in its lift. Wash it down and take
care of more maintenance chores. Go back to your
quarters for a cocktail, perhaps, and dinner. Watch TV
or write letters and go to bed. The spiral of fatigue is
never-ending, especially if the boat is not doing well.

Ed Adams, a great collegiate dinghy racer and observer of the racing scene, has pointed out that "the
problem with all campaigns—and it's certainly true of
America's Cup and Olympic competition—is that by
the end of the campaign you have been at it so long
that unless you win, and sometimes even if you do,
crews can be angry with each other or aren't talking;
they're just tired of being together under stress for such
a long time. It takes special people to be able to get
along."

Another interesting point hidden in Robinson's account is the sophistication of the gear aboard *Defender*

as compared with that on *Courageous* six years earlier.
As much as a quantum leap may have occurred between 1983 and 1987.

Courageous of 1977 was nothing like *Defender,* or today's twelve-meter. There was one position for the mast,
three different settings for the running backstays. Jib
leads could not be moved easily. The sails were all made
of Dacron; some were lighter and fuller and some were
flatter and heavier.

Most of the modern twelves are like Leggo blocks;
the variables are almost infinite. You can shift the mast
forward and aft with unlimited settings. Jib leads can
be instantly changed forward, aft, inboard, and outboard on call. Computerized instruments give you precise rates of acceleration in tiny increments and also can
call up the comparative acceleration of a previous tack
and the time it took to accomplish it. Onboard computers transmit information on everything the twelve
does to other computers aboard tenders that provide
instant analysis to the skippers if the boat is practicing,
or for review in the evening if the boat is racing. Every
race is taped by videocameras aboard the tenders and
watched religiously by crews at night. In 1983 I ana-
lyzed the videotapes every evening and made notes to
be discussed with the crew the following day.

Design methods have changed radically, too. Tank
testing was a norm, but not to be totally depended upon.
The tank's computer printouts were only a guide, as
Olin Stephens once said, but "intuition and experience
are necessary to interpret them correctly." This year,
the French Cup challenger, *French Kiss,* is the result of
some very sophisticated modeling on the computers of
the French jet fighter manufacturer Dassault. It was
never tank-tested; the computer had ingested enormous numbers of variables, compared a great many

designs, and came up with what the French felt was an optimum boat that promptly went into production. There is one variable, however, that defies computerization, and that is the quality, composition, and experience of the crew. A boat can be fast, but if the crew is slow, disorganized, or mechanically inept, it will never make the cut.

Playing the variables, both mechanical and political, was the hard lesson I learned as one of the principals in the 1983 *Defender-Courageous* campaign to unseat Dennis Conner as the potential Cup defender.

Californian Tom Blackaller, unvanquished in six meters and twice world champion in the hard-to-sail Stars, and I had been the prime movers behind getting a new twelve built to team up with a reconstructed *Courageous* in an attempt to do battle with *Australia II* in defense of the Cup. We had been relentless in trying to raise money to get the effort started, and after fifteen months we finally got a commitment from a young couple, Nick and Jane Heyl, to finance the design and construction of the twelve that eventually was to be known as *Defender*. The move precipitated the formation of the *Defender-Courageous* Syndicate, a kind of amalgam of factions interested in stopping Dennis Conner, who was returning with a new twelve, the big red *Liberty,* after successfully defending the Cup in 1980.

The late yacht designer and historian Howard L. Chapelle once wrote that "the design of a yacht is a matter of compromising conflicting elements . . . the fewer the compromises the better the design will be."

Whereas the designer of a cruising boat has to juggle requirements for accommodations—boat speed, the ability to weather big seas, and ease of handling—the

twelve-meter designer has a more severe problem—
trying to develop a boat to solve a syndicate's wishes
within a rule that is like a rubber suit. If you stretch it
in one place, it must contract in another. Another factor in twelve-meter design is that the America's Cup is
not only a race to uphold national prestige but a derby
for the naval architect as well. Failure to produce a
winning twelve-meter is not a happy prospect for the
designer; perhaps two years have been devoted to the
project to the detriment of other paying work in the
shop for a gamble on a jackpot if the boat wins and
obscurity if it loses. In 1983, each designer lived or died
with one boat. In 1987, many of the syndicates were
in Fremantle with three or four vessels—each supposedly better than the other so the odds were more in the
designer's favor.

In *Defender*'s case, Dave Pedrick, who had been very
closely associated with Sparkman & Stephens and who
had worked on other twelve-meter designs, was offered the opportunity to take the risk and come up with
a winning twelve. Pedrick signed the contract in August 1981 and was given his lead to design a boat that
would accelerate a little faster and point a little higher
than the twelves on the scene. Pedrick disappeared into
his studio in Newport to work the "black art" (as a
noted designer has described it), calling us only to ask
questions about deck layout. "Just leave him alone, he's
working," Tom Blackaller said to me once when I
wanted to call Pedrick.

In November 1981 we did meet under mysterious
circumstances in an old shed at Cove Haven near Barrington, R.I., where several twelves had been stored.
Here under cover were at least four of the twelves—
Courageous, Freedom, the British *Lionheart,* and the

Swedish *Sverige,* all of which had competed in 1980. It was a ghostly place. One could easily imagine life aboard those boats, tacticians and skippers and trimmers at work, all calling to each other as they headed for some phantom mark.

We were there, in fact, to resurrect the crews; we pulled the covers back on all the boats to study their deck layouts and crew positions and to make our own modifications for *Defender.*

Pedrick's next move was to transfer his drawings into models, which then were tank-tested to see how the hull form behaved at various speed and heeling angles under a number of different wave conditions. About $175,000 was spent on tank testing. The same "leave him alone" philosophy kept us away from the tank tests, so that the first time we saw the finished drawings, all the studies had been done. Pedrick predicted the boat would be faster than *Courageous* except in the windiest conditions. (It wasn't. It struggled in a seaway with too much sail area and not enough stability.)

We approved the plans, however, and construction started in February 1982 at Newport Offshore, in Newport. First Pedrick's drawings were "lofted," the lines of the boat enlarged many times and transferred to a large, white-painted area of the floor so that the boat's aluminum frames and other integral parts of the hull could be fabricated. Then the boat's skeleton was constructed, the hull was covered with aluminum plates, and it took on the shape that Pedrick had designed for it. And then the project visibly slowed down as various pieces of gear didn't arrive on schedule. Worst of all was a five-week delay in delivery of the mast, which lost us a month or more of sailing time.

We sailed *Defender* as much as we could that summer

and fall of 1982, until she was dismasted, at which point she was stored and then shipped to California for trials against *Courageous* in the spring. It was suspected that the boat was a problem child, first in California, then after returning to Newport in June 1983. But when it came to modifying the boat, we ran into a wall at the syndicate, as did Pedrick, who wanted some study time to decide what changes could be made. Reported Pedrick, "They didn't let me do the job I needed to do to make the corrections." Said a member of the syndicate, "Well, he should have done it right in the first place."

In retrospect, one remarkable achievement was the fact that Blackaller and I were the first in the long history of the Cup to come out of the ranks, as it were, to develop a twelve. But, mistakenly, as it turned out, we skewed *Defender* toward light air. If *Courageous* did her best in fourteen-knot breezes, we were looking for a boat that really would be fast at about 10½ knots true wind speed. The theory was that the boat ought to be quick in light and medium air and that our great sailing ability and crew work would overcome the heavy-air problem.

With our experience we should have recognized that during America's Cup summers, the crews get so good at handling sails under any wind conditions that crew work ceases to be a factor but boat speed is.

There were other design factors incorporated in the boat that also were based on misconceptions. *Defender* was too short on the waterline. At the same time, she was the widest twelve-meter built up to that time, with a beam of twelve feet, eight inches. (Most twelves are about twelve feet to twelve feet, four inches wide). Here the thinking was that if you flared out the topsides, when the boat was heeled it would help boat speed by making it appear in the water that the waterline was longer than it actually was. Also, we figured that wider beam would allow us to put our jib leads more outboard. But we learned that since so little time is spent reaching with a headsail, we had penalized ourselves unnecessarily. It was all a calculated risk.

As it turned out, by the end of the summer, the racing became emotionless; if it was blowing over thirteen knots, *Defender* didn't have a chance. If the wind dropped to eleven knots, *Defender* probably would win. But to race in the America's Cup, you need an all-around boat, one with speed in every sort of condition, and we were "excused" by the selection committee, who gave Conner and *Liberty* the nod.

In the meantime we were learning something about the politics of the game. Some strange things happened that spring and summer.

All of the boats, Conner's two—*Freedom* (which had successfully defended the Cup in 1980) and *Liberty*—and our two, *Defender* and *Courageous,* were trial racing in California during the spring, but no races were held among the four boats. Had they been held, deficiencies such as *Defender*'s inability to move upwind in heavy air, or *Liberty*'s slow speed downwind, might have been corrected.

Very few trial races among the Americans were run on the America's Cup course, while the foreign challengers were in the area every day. At Newport, as you move away from shore, the current decreases and the wind, under less influence from the land, is southerly rather than southwesterly. *Defender* raced on the course only twice the entire summer and never had the chance to run the full four-hour, twenty-four-mile route, which always is a test of dealing with changing conditions and wind shifts.

But perhaps the biggest disappointment of all was learning from the Australians rather than the proper source (either the Conner group or the selection committee) that *Liberty* was being run under different measurement certificates each day to try out certain variables. It is not illegal to change measurements between races, but the other syndicates are meant to be notified by 9:00 P.M. the previous evening.

One day we would be blazing fast downwind against *Liberty,* and the next day, with the same crew, same wind, same sails, we would lose a minute on a run. Finally the Aussies, who had their own intelligence-gathering operation, leaked it to the press. We saw *Liberty's* hull when the July trials ended, discovered the three measurement marks, and began to understand what was going on. Our heated protest to the selection committee brought a response from its chairman that set the tone for the rest of the summer: "We'd like to keep this a secret, because it's an edge that we have against the Australians." What he was really saying was that after all of our fund-raising efforts and the agony of bringing a new twelve to life, we were really acting as a trial horse for *Liberty.*

If it was true, as Conner had said, that the America's Cup was "a game of life," then someone else was controlling the score.

5

YACHTSMEN

*I*n the world of sailing, the word "true" is used frequently. We have true or geographic north. We take a true bearing on an object at sea—the direction of that object, perhaps a boat or a navigation aid, on the compass in terms of true north. We have "true" wind, the direction of the wind before it arrives at the boat and is confused by boat speed and becomes "apparent" wind.

In this section you will meet some true yachtsmen, people in sailing who have been intensely involved with the sport but whose horizon is as wide as the ocean's. They have offered me a sense of direction and have not held back in allowing me the free use of their experience. Owners, skippers, crewmates, and friends, they have known where north is, truly.

HERBERT VON KARAJAN:
Maestro

Herbert von Karajan stepped on board his yacht and raised his arms. His crew, acting in concert, prepared the boat for getting under way, singled up the lines, and we cast off the dock at St. Tropez for our first sail together.

Exhausted from a sleepless night on a flight from the States, I quietly took it all in—this small (five-six), well-tanned, compactly built person taking charge of his vessel just as easily as he commands the famed Berlin Philharmonic. Then, noticing that I was on board, too, he said, "Gary, we know what you are all about. Your reputation has preceded you. My goal is to have perfection in this crew, and your job is to help carry this out."

It was July 1979. The maestro, Herbert von Karajan, had invited me to help train the crew of his thirty-nine-foot, Ron Holland-designed *Helisara V*. Dick Bertram, a fierce competitor in sail and power, had suggested that I contact von Karajan. Bertram and I had crewed together the previous summer aboard the maxiracer *Ondine* during the Big Boat Series in San Francisco Bay. "It would be good for you, Gary," Bertram said, "and it would be good for him. I can arrange it."

The idea of sailing with von Karajan, one of the world's best known and most influential musicians, and yet, in his seventies, a true sportsman who piloted his own jet, skied like a devil, and commanded his own racing yacht, appealed to me. Perhaps there was something I could learn from this gentleman, whose concerts drew standing ovations in his native Berlin and, indeed, everywhere he conducted. Friends described him as tough (he would need to be), but his letters belied it. Our correspondence, which still continues, had a formal beginning in November 1978:

> Dear Mr. Jobson.
> Thank you very much for your letter.
> Needless to say it would be a great honor to have the best sailor . . . in the world giving us his advice and training.
> Yours sincerely,
> Herbert von Karajan

The letter had been dictated to his secretary at his office in Salzburg, Austria, while he was typically on the fly. But he also wrote that he was commissioning Argentinian designer German Frers to design a new seventy-seven-foot maxiracer for him and that he owned a C&C 61 that was being outclassed, so in the interim he had ordered the Holland-designed sloop from Nautor of Finland. The boat would be delivered in St. Tropez in the late spring or early summer, where later correspondence directed me to join it.

Now, on the first day of sailing with the maestro and his crew, I decided I would observe and then make suggestions. "They would like to be pushed to their limits," von Karajan had said, and gradually we began doing just that after instruction in English and "Franglish" (broken French) in improving tacks, making better jibes, and improving their spinnaker techniques. I went through each function step by step. It was fun for the crew, who had been spending their afternoons "going sailing" with the maestro, which is not the same as hard-nosed boathandling, especially with the possibility of racing in mind.

The routine was simple. Von Karajan came abroad precisely at 2:00 P.M. At 6:00 P.M. the boat was back at the dock. So every afternoon for those four hours we would sail out of St. Tropez, our minuscule thirty-nine-footer threading its way among the magnificent power yachts of the rich and famous. I had coached the crew in the morning. When von Karajan stepped aboard, we were ready to work. The maestro would take the helm—hoping for perfection out of the crew, the same sort of unison he expected out of his orchestra. At the helm, he was in a familiar role—the conductor of a group of persons who would create the perfection of sailing. Like orchestral music, sailing a large boat takes considerable practice and teamwork. Each person is critical to the whole operation; everyone suffers if there is a foul-up.

Making smooth tacks and reach-to-reach jibes was difficult at first, but within a day the mostly French crew was able to go through each maneuver smoothly in winds up to twenty-five knots. St. Tropez, as with most of the French Riviera between Monte Carlo and Hyères, enjoys an afternoon thermal. The wind starts out at zero early in the morning and by afternoon works its way up to twenty-five.

Under these afternoon conditions the crew was pushed to its utmost, sometimes doing twenty jibes followed by forward spinnaker takedowns and multiple tacks before setting the spinnaker. Performance improved each day, and by the fourth day we were able to maneuver *Helisara* as well as any topflight racing boat. On the beach sat von Karajan's French wife, and it seemed as if he were proudly performing for her as much as for himself as he directed the movements of *Helisara*.

One crew member was von Karajan's friend Gianni Agnelli, the president of Fiat (later a backer of the Italian twelve-meter effort in 1983). He had a perfect British accent and worked in the cockpit trimming sails like everyone else. Then at the end of the day of sailing we dropped him off at his 190-foot power yacht anchored in the harbor.

My one regret when the week ended and I departed *Helisara* is that I did not get to know von Karajan better. There were none of the long talks I expected to have with him about his world, which was so different from mine. There was no language barrier and he wasn't cold, but it was all business—the business of sailing.

Salzburg 1979/07/20

My dear Gary,
The day you left there was a big void on *Helisara*. My boys simply could not take it that you were not with us anymore.
You really opened a new world in sailing and I think my crew was conscious of that. Anyhow they did not want to disappoint you and [finished] in 3rd place elapsed time in a 20 boat fleet in the Giraglia race. Not too bad, isn't it?

Yours,
Herbert von Karajan

Salzburg 1979/12/20

My dear Gary,
Excuse me for being so late. I had an enormous program to do, including a concert tour of Japan and China. My crew and I have been talking much about

you and you seem to be with us personally present. When we have a problem, we always ask ourselves what you would have done.

Now, good luck for you, Merry Christmas and all good wishes.

Yours,
Herbert von Karajan

This was the winter that von Karajan's new seventy-seven-foot maxi racer was built at the Huisman Yard in Holland. It was also the winter I signed up for the 1980 America's Cup defense by *Courageous* and was totally occupied that spring, summer, and fall as a member of its crew. I corresponded with the maestro about details of his new boat but never made it to Europe to sail with him that year.

Salzburg 1980/06/24

Dear Gary,

The new *Helisara* is on her way to St. Tropez. She is full of possibilities and certainly needs time to get known. I confidently hope for your help next year.

I realize you are busy now in training. I have read with great interest about your preparation and in the name of the crew and myself, all our best wishes for the races.

Best regards,
Herbert von Karajan

With the 1980 America's Cup tucked away (but not by *Courageous*), there was time to think about *Helisara* and its owner. More letters went back and forth, von Karajan again communicating with me on the fly between concert trips. Salzburg was his mail drop; he'd pick up his mail, then dictate a reply to his secretary, then leave for another concert trip. More than one letter was signed by a lady identified only as Ms. Salzberger, with the note "Herbert von Karajan, left after dictation."

In December 1980 he wrote:

Now about the both of us.
Will you have the time to come to Europe next summer? . . . We will have our crew more or less together on June 15. It would be a great help and an immense joy if you could come any time after this period.

It was an offer I couldn't refuse and in early July I found myself again in St. Tropez. But this time, our relationship had subtly changed to something warmer, although still totally professional. The new boat, *Helisara V,* is a beauty from the board of German Frers. I had no idea how it would really sail because von Karajan still was not commited to major racing. But with the larger boat I was more effective in organizing the crew, and along with the training I decided to convince the maestro to enter the Maxi worlds in Sardinia in September.

Again we sailed every afternoon from 2:00 to 6:00 P.M. after crew training in the morning. Again von Karajan, at the helm, demanded perfection—jibes that went perfectly, tacks that were unflawed. Speed is his fetish, and there is nothing he liked better than finding some thirty-five-foot cruising boat and passing it with unerring speed—"blasting over the top," as the racers say. One of his daughters, Isabella, a student in acting, sailed with us and was a great favorite of the mostly French crew. Again Gianni Agnelli took his place at the cock-pit winch, and von Karajan played host as well to Hel-mut Schmidt, ex-chancellor of West Germany. Every afternoon at the maestro's command we maneuvered around the buoys, getting better and better at it as the week progressed.

Onshore the maestro sped around the resort in his turbo Renault and we found ourselves spending more personal time together. There was dinner one evening at his house—a lovely large stucco place on the bay—where I broached the idea of entering *Helisara* in the Maxi Worlds in Sardinia. "It will give your crew something to really train for," I said. "A sense of pur-pose." The challenge of putting *Helisara* up against the world's biggest and fastest racing yachts appealed to him. "Yes," he said, enthusiastically, "we'll do it if you come and help us."

Later that month he wrote:

It was nice to have you with us and . . . the crew and myself feel better about what we are doing. We were all very sad the day you left us.

A few days later, *Helisara* won the prestigious Gir-aglia race, coming in five hours ahead of the second-place finisher. In a postscript to his letter, von Karajan penned "HURRAH!"

Now, in early September, Janice and I wait in the air terminal in Zurich for the maestro to arrive and fly us and some of his entourage in his Falcon jet to Sardinia, where *Helisara* and its crew await our arrival. He walks in briskly, smiles and greets us warmly, and then says,

"Gary, I think we are in for the battle of our lives." I reassure him, "It's not like we've never sailed together before. We'll see how it goes."

Privately I know that *Helisara* has never been put to the extreme test of racing the best there is in the off-shore world. I have no idea how fast the boat really is, although I suspect that with the Frers credentials and what I have seen of her maneuverability she may surprise us all. On the flight down, little is said; von Karajan concentrates on flying the plane, a chore he takes very seriously. He is very good, putting the plane down at Porto Cervo, as he describes it, "like a butterfly with sore feet."

The Maxi Worlds are hosted by the Aga Khan at his Costa Smeralda resort, and von Karajan is putting us up at one of the more beautiful hotels. But even more beautiful, if not threatening, is the assemblage of big racing yachts and their professional crews in the harbor.

Ondine is there. The brand-new eighty-foot *Kialoa* is there, and so is the eighty-one-foot *Condor,* with Dennis Conner at the helm. The seventy-eight-foot *Xargo* is geared up with sailmaker and twelve-meter racer Robby Doyle and California's Dennis Durgin.

There is a lot of competition among the thirteen maxis. "We are going to have to hustle," I tell the crew as we begin practicing.

But hustling doesn't seem to be part of their routine, which is to sail out with wine and cheese, do some maneuvering, and head back—as if they are cruising.

After the first day I tell them, "No more wine and cheese. We want to be hungry and work hard." There is no grumbling. Most of them had sailed with me in July, and I know they can be psyched enough to do their best. By this time I am "sailing in French." I can't speak the language, but I know all the sailing terms and can use them to give the appropriate commands. Whatever I want to do is all right with von Karajan, who can hardly disguise his desire to win.

In the first race we're over the line early at the start and are involved in a protest situation. But despite the miscue, we finish fifth and survive the protest. Fifth out of thirteen boats is an excellent way to begin for an untried crew, and everyone feels heartened.

In the next two days we do better and better and I realize that *Helisara* really is fast, that the crew is working together like a von Karajan orchestra, and that we stand a chance of doing very well in the series. In fact, we place second and third in succeeding races.

The final race is a long-distance affair of some 160 miles, beating up along the north coast of Sardinia through the Strait of Bonifacio between Sardinia and Corsica to the Gulf of Asinara, where there is a turning mark for home. We start out very competitively with a fair breeze until we reach the Gulf of Asinara and round the buoy. Then the wind dies, and the top five maxis are together—*Ondine, Kialoa, Bumblebee, Helisara,* and *Xargo.*

Von Karajan never leaves the deck. He takes many roles—part-time tactician, helmsman, the general of the crew. He never goes below during the entire twenty-four-hour race. We have arrived, along with the other becalmed boats in the Gulf of Asinara, in the early evening, but during the night, I keep the crew moving. I know from experience that races are won or lost during the night because of inattention to trim and sail changing. During the night, however, the crew does its job to keep the boat moving. We are able to pick up some wind shifts and flee the calm area.

When the sun comes up, we are about a mile behind *Kialoa,* and the two of us are light-years ahead of the rest of the fleet. All day long the breeze comes up as we sail downwind chasing *Kialoa.* We are "bringing up the new breeze" in the jargon of offshore racing and finally are close enough to her to begin a one-on-one jibing duel, which lasts for fifty miles.

The maestro loves every minute of it. We continue to gain on them. Our jibes are better as their chute collapses and there are some signs of dissolution on *Kialoa.* A great deal of yelling can be heard from Harold Cudmore, the skipper. The more nervous the *Kialoa* crew seems, the more spirited ours gets, until about three miles from the finish line we overtake *Kialoa* and beat them by fifty-five seconds. "Bravo!" shouts the maestro, his hands clenched in the air, tears streaming down his face. "Bravo!"

There is a great celebration that night in Costa Smeralda, with von Karajan proudly receiving his trophy from the Aga Khan. It is one of the proudest moments for a man who spends much of his life taking applause for work well done. But this, somehow, is different.

BUDDY MELGES:
The Wizard of Zenda

At age fifteen, my heroes were all local ones. I was totally involved with sailing on Barnegat Bay, and the men I admired most were Barnegat Bay sailors who hardly ever lost and who always had time to talk to a skinny adolescent kid who wondered if he would ever be as good at racing as they were. Sometimes they would ask me to crew for them, and that would be a magic day in my life.

Among my heroes was Runyon Colie, Jr., one of the first of the great collegiate dinghy racers. Colie spent his summers at Barnegat Bay, raced an E-scow, and always finished at the top of the fleet. Colie took me in hand later and showed me that concentration and constant practice sailing around the buoys would help me improve my racing skills.

My other heroes were Sam Merrick and Tom Chapman, also constant winners on the bay. It never occurred to me that these men were vulnerable and could be beaten until that summer of 1965, when Harry (Buddy) Melges arrived at Little Egg Harbor for the E-scow Nationals, which were held at Barnegat Bay that year.

I knew that Melges had won an Olympic bronze in Flying Dutchmen dinghies the year before in Japan and the Mallory Cup three times, but I'm not sure I was aware that, at thirty-five, he had already won the Inland Lake E-scow championships four times and the C-scows, on his turf, twice.

Buddy Melges, whose tongue was reputed to be as sharp as his sailing, was a hot ticket, probably the best dinghy racer in the country. But Barnegat Bay was the eastern center for scow racing, and it was thought that the locals could hold their own against anyone.

They didn't have a chance against Melges and his midwestern crew, who demolished the local fleet, including all my heroes, by winning almost every race.

Melges's strategy was completely different from anything any of us had seen on the bay before.

While sailing on a run, most of our boats pulled their

spinnaker poles all of the way aft and ran dead down-wind. Melges showed up with a flat-reaching spinna-ker and reached back and forth across the course on the leeward legs, gaining speed on each reach. It was a technique one might use on a catamaran or an iceboat. And as Melges also was a distinguished iceboat sailor (eleven championships over the years), you could see the cross-pollination at work.

While I was away at college and entering my sailing career, Melges was amassing a record in small-boat racing that still is unequaled. He was named Yachts-man of the Year three times and won more national and world titles than any living American, including an Olympic gold medal in Solings in 1972.

Legends abound about Melges. He is so good at sail-ing, with a natural feel for tactics and possessing great physical strength, that he can sail any boat well, even the unfamiliar ones, thereby confounding the skeptics.

In 1972, never having had much experience with Solings (a twenty-eight foot keelboat sloop), Melges showed up at the Olympic Solings trials in San Fran-cisco. The series was held in typical windy weather, and on the first day he placed fifth after a premature start, followed by a dismasting in the second race. Most sailors would have packed up their boat and headed home. But not Melges. He spent a good part of the night rigging a new mast, then went on to win five straight races, securing a berth for the Olympics. At Kiel, against an assembly of national champions and their battle-trained crews, he won the gold in an amaz-ing series of victories.

Later he performed a similar feat in Star boats. Clas-sic in their looks, Stars are one of the oldest one-design classes in the world. They were first raced before the turn of the century, and today every major America's Cup skipper has competed in Stars—tough, sloop-rigged boats that demand the best of their crews.

In 1978 Melges decided that his record wouldn't be complete until he took up Star sailing. He hadn't been in one, but he looked at the sails (he was a sailmaker as well as a boatbuilder), made some innovations in the rig, and took himself and his new boat to the Star Worlds in San Francisco Bay.

In the parking lot on the day before the first race, Melges met Dennis Conner, Star sailor of some repute, who said, "It's too bad you have to sail with your own sails," obviously thinking that Melges's "homemade" jobs wouldn't be able to go the route against the Norths and Hoods and others that the racers were using. "Well," replied Melges, "we'll just have a go at it and see what happens."

In the first race, Melges rounded the first mark more than two minutes ahead of Conner and the local champion, Tom Blackaller. Melges went on to win the series without having to race the last race, never looking back. After the regatta had ended, Melges asked Conner, "Would you like to borrow my sails to race with? I know the guy who makes them and I can get you a good deal." There is no record of Conner's reply.

You can imagine my feelings when Melges, seventeen years after I first admired him during those fateful days on Barnegat Bay, agreed to enter the Hall of Fame regatta in 1982 (see pages 107–111). The possibility of losing to him and a crew of his two sons, Harry, Jr., and Hans, always was present. In fact, they came in second, and my notes show, "He is extremely tough and likes to take chances. . . . He is always the first to port tack the fleet or go for the gold. It catches up with him, and in many of his major events he has had a

DNF (Did Not Finish) to carry, but his ability and his aggressiveness always come through."

I finally had the opportunity to see Melges close up when I was invited not long ago to race with him aboard his A-scow in Madison, Wis. Twenty-two of these thirty-eight-foot dish-bottomed sloops, the ultimate in the breed, had congregated for the regatta on Lake Mendota. On the first day of racing, which I missed, Melges, sailing a borrowed boat (he had loaned his own to a friend), had placed fourth and fifth. On this particular day, on the way out to the starting line, Melges gave us a pep talk. "I'm counting on you to win," he said.

It was the first time I had actually raced in the same boat with Melges, and I discovered that he was every bit as good a skipper as I thought he was. This is something that is never apparent from off the boat. Clearly Melges was a natural sailor, but he had other attributes; he had the finesse of a brain surgeon in trimming the sails, and even at fifty-six, he had excellent eyesight and was hawklike at picking up wind shifts. He also had a good sense of the course, knowing where we were at every moment in relation to the other boats. Although heavier than he was in 1965, he is still very strong, with massive arms and a full body.

An A-scow weighs eighteen hundred pounds, sails with a masthead spinnaker, and may be the fastest monohull in the world. But provided we did our jobs, Melges made it look easy. Doing our jobs meant intense concentration; he won't tolerate less than that. I was able to give him input, but it had to be done in a nonadversarial manner. No one talks back to Captain Melges on board; he will explode in anger and, perhaps, apologize later.

Melges, I noticed, is not one of the secret sailors. He

is a good teacher and loves to counsel others on technique, boatbuilding, and sail trim. During the weekend regatta he made a point of sailing with other competitors between races and made sure that our crew understood how to sail his boat while he was not on board.

In the end, we placed second for the series, but for the hardworking Melges, the sailing hadn't ended yet. He had the boat towed back to his home waters at the little town of Zenda (population, fifty) on Lake Geneva, where he rerigged the scow and tested two mainsails.

The biggest thing in Zenda is the Melges Boatworks, which has been doing business in the town for several generations and employs many of the local folks. It still is a family-run concern. Both grown sons, Harry, Jr., and Hans, are very much a part of it. We arrived after the race at Melges's Victorian-era house in his aged white Mercedes convertible. He was relaxed now that he was off the boat and business for the day had come to an end.

That evening began a new association with Buddy Melges that still continues. He has taken on the skippership of the Chicago-based Heart of America Challenge for the America's Cup. As a consultant to the group I watched him function in this new role as both observer (at the twelve-meter Worlds) and commander (on board *Heart of America*). He has never been a twelve-meter skipper before, and at Fremantle he will be a long way from Zenda.

But it won't matter because he is the wizard.

CONN FINDLAY:
Glue of the Crew

Every racing sailboat has one person around whom the
boat and the crew revolves. If a boat is a cell (sometimes it seems that way), that person is the nucleus.
He is not the skipper but the one person on board who
not only is a splendid sailor and can handle any job on
deck but who also can fix practically anything that
breaks. If I were writing a help-wanted ad, I would
probably say:

> Crewperson needed for U.S. America's Cup
> yacht now being tested off Western Australia. Must
> be qualified to fill any crew position but particu-
> larly looking for mastman. Ability with tools a
> prerequisite. Must be in excellent physical condi-
> tion. Report to Fishing Harbour, Fremantle.

I go on to imagine a quiet knock on the syndicate
office door some days later and there would stand a
giant, the Paul Bunyan of yachting. Conn Findlay has
arrived. How he has gotten there, you don't know.
And you don't inquire. With almost two decades of
offshore racing experience, his physical strength, his six-
seven height ("I'm really five-nineteen"), he is just what
you want for one of the most difficult jobs on board.
Being the mastman takes strength because he handles
the halyards and the spinnaker pole, but he also must

be alert to potential disaster on the foredeck and be able to jump in to help very quickly.

Findlay, in his early fifties, has been a fixture on world-class and America's Cup yachts ever since I've been involved with big boats. Not many know, however, that his greatest fame came in rowing in the Olympics, where he won two golds and a bronze in 1956, 1960, and 1964 in double sculls. He still is involved with the sport, leasing rowing shells to universities and rowing clubs on the West Coast. "I own more sixty-footers than anyone in the world," he'll tell you, referring to his shells.

A native Californian, Findlay nominally makes his home in Belmont, near San Francisco, when he is not racing. But getting him to race with you is not always so easy. In 1980, just after spending a frustrating summer in Newport aboard *Courageous,* I turned up in San Francisco for the Big Boat Series with a berth on *Mistress Quickly*. All of the glamorous vessels were there— *Windward Passage, Kialoa,* and others. Findlay came to the dock, looked around, said "I'm going fishing," and departed.

There are as many stories about Conn Findlay as there are about the legendary Paul Bunyan. In 1976 Findlay crewed with Dennis Conner aboard a Tempest in the Olympics. On the final beat in the last race, they had a chance to gamble for a silver medal and come in second if they split tacks with the boat leading them and got to the finish line ahead. Missing on the tack would put them fourth. The alternative was to cover and get an automatic bronze. "Well, Conn," said Conner, "should we go for the silver or stay with the bronze?" From the trapeze came Findlay's reply, "I've got MY medals." Conner did not take the chance and they took third place.

"Life is perfect," Findlay said to me once, "when you have no checkbook." He asked me, "Gary, how many checks do you write a month?" Then he answered his own question. "The fewer checks you have to write each month, the better organized your life is." I said, "Conn, how many checks are you writing each month?" He replied, "Zero. I don't have a checking account. I pay for everything with cash."

In 1977 Findlay served as mastman on *Courageous*. But for him, being a member of the crew didn't stop when he came off the boat. He was always first up in the morning, working out and then going down to the boat to help get repairs made and the boat ready for sailing.

On board as we practiced and raced in Newport, Findlay was quiet, seeming without emotion, but very quick to move when things seemed hopelessly fouled. Coming into a leeward mark, with the chute still up, the jib halfway up, and the pole on the wrong side of the headstay, it seemed as if we would never get out of the mess we were in. Suddenly there Findlay was on the foredeck of the twelve-meter, sorting it out smoothly and quickly. He was so strong that he seemed to overpower the situation.

It went like that the entire summer of 1977 as *Courageous* competed for the defender's slot. There were the emotional mood swings of winning in June, losing in July, then winning in August and sweeping into the Cup. And even during the cup races, the most important events in yachting, Findlay calmly went about his business, never revealing his feelings, even after the third race, when for the third time we defeated *Australia* and it was apparent that we were going to take it all. Finally, after crossing the finish line first in the fourth race to the cheers and horns of the assembled boats, Findlay put his arms around me and gave me a kind of bear hug and danced on the deck. I knew then that all summer he had been keeping his feelings bottled up because steadiness is what it's all about when you are the glue of the crew.

GEORGE COUMANTAROS:
Style and Substance

We mentioned earlier that there are owners and there are yachtsmen. George Coumantaros is a yachtsman, a gentleman who races hard and is fond of winning but who also is one of those rare persons—an honorable man. I had the good fortune to sail with him aboard his sixty-five-foot Derecktor-built yacht *Boomerang* for two years and learned the meaning of the word "class."

Coumantaros's Greek heritage must have led him to the sea. An enormously wealthy shipowner (27 ships at last count), he has been involved with racing for many years. His seventy-three-foot ketch *Baccara,* built during the last days of the Cruising Club of America (CCA) Rule, always was a feature of the Class A fleet of most major regattas, including the SORC. He never really was able to put a string of victories together with *Baccara,* although he may have had the satisfaction of knowing she was one of the most admired vessels in the racing fleets. Not only was the boat beautiful, but Coumantaros also set a good table; his crews always have been well fed.

When CCA went out and IOR came in with its studied, beamy boats and relatively short ends (unlike the graceful overhangs of CCA), Coumantaros had

Boomerang designed and built to replace *Baccara,* which suddenly had become obsolete. Coumantaros has always believed that he was never warned quickly enough about the change from CCA to IOR, even though his designer, Olin Stephens, knew that the IOR was coming. Had Coumantaros known he might not have built *Baccara,* he has said.

Coumantaros, known by his crew as "Cou," divides his time when he is not racing between a large apartment in New York City and a home in Greenwich, Conn. In both places hang original art work he has been collecting for years. His career began when his father moved to Argentina from Greece after World War II and started a shipping company with which Coumantaros still is involved. He is in the business of moving grain and wheat out of Nigeria aboard his ships. He also owns a Löwenbräu brewery in Italy.

The other side of his life is yachting; he always has been involved with the New York Yacht Club, and he has helped finance several twelve-meter syndicates.

One of them was ours, the 1983 *Defender-Courageous* group. We had approached him in his office, knowing of his philanthropies in yachting, with a budget of $2.7 million. "You are misrepresenting the facts," he said. "How are you going to beat Conner with two point seven million dollars? Go away, and when you come back with an organized plan, I'll talk with you."

In the late spring of that year (1982), we went back to him aboard *Boomerang* in Newport, where he was awaiting word that the heavy weather had passed and that there would indeed be a Bermuda Race. This time we showed him what a realistic budget of four million dollars would do for the syndicate. Coumantaros took it all in and then said, "This is going to be a very expensive postponement." He reached into his wallet and took out a creased, folded personal check and spread it out on the dining table. "How do I make this out?" he asked. We told him and he wrote out a check to the People to People Foundation for one hundred thousand dollars.

In the Maxi-Worlds in Newport in 1985 it came down to one race. Sailing as tactician with Bill Koch on *Matador,* we were tied with *Boomerang* with three wins apiece. At the last leeward mark *Matador* was leading by a boat length when her mast collapsed and she had to drop out of the race. *Boomerang* went on to win the race and the regatta.

At the trophy ceremony Coumantaros said, "We are really happy to win, but there will always be a question in our minds: Which is the better boat? On this day it just happened that our number turned up." That was the Coumantaros style. It would not have been like him to take the trophy and run.

TED TURNER:
The South Rises Again

> Some people are born fleet of foot,
> make great runners. When basic characteristics
> were doled out, I got more than my share of
> competitiveness. That's probably all.
> In fact, it may not be all that healthy.
>
> Ted Turner

At Sea with Ted

There was always something about Turner and his boats that drew people into wanting to sail with him. He was a winner and therefore attracted the best sailors, who may have doubted his ability on the course early on but who watched him trialed by fire at SORC and other world events, became believers, and sailed with him for a long time. They found that sloppiness was not in his makeup, that despite his flamboyance ashore, at sea he ran a taut, safe ship.

Sailing with Turner was not for the sensitive or the thin-skinned. There were risks, and mostly they were caused by his quick and often scathing humor. If you were an old hand, you disregarded it and went about your work; but if you were a new hotshot young recruit from the collegiate sailing ranks, at some point early in the race you would be a victim of the Turner tongue.

It didn't help if you were a collegiate champion or even an Olympic medal winner. Turner was a master at hazing the best in a ritual he obviously had learned at the military school he had attended from age five.

"Trim, trim, trim," he would yell, "you're so fat that your stomach is getting in the way!" The new boy would make a mistake. Perhaps in trimming the spinnaker sheet he would lose the curl so that the chute would begin to collapse. Ted would roar at him, "Where the hell did you learn how to sail?"

The recruit always went through it alone, with no response or help from the rest of the crew, many of whom had been through it themselves. Turner's theory, once you understood it, was simple—the old Marine game of break the guy down, see if he can take it, and build him up so that he works even harder for you.

Forty-five minutes after the tirade, both Turner and the new crewman might be below. He would try to avoid Turner, but the skipper would say, "Well, you're getting the hang of it. There might be hope for you yet." Now the young sailor wanted to be on board so badly that if Turner asked, he would cut off the Turk's Head rope bracelet he'd been wearing on his wrist since he was thirteen.

Actually, Turner was a realist about his crews, knew that mistakes were possible, and said to me during one of the discussions we always seemed to be having when we sailed together, "The chance for mistakes is about equal to the number of crew squared, so that every additional crew member increases that percentage." But Turner's forte was his ability to minimize mistakes through finding good sailors who would get along well together, enjoyed sailing with each other, and were secure enough in their own abilities to deal with him as well. Turner is a master at organization, and it showed up on all of his boats, particularly *Tenacious,* which had, more or less, the same crew for more than four years. "Your greatest premium," he said, "is on organization

and recruiting, just like it is in basketball and baseball
. . . having the experience to know what kind of
equipment to get and who to put your money on."

Turner's sense of organization extended not only to
crew but to how the boat was managed and sailed as
well. Let's say that a race is to begin on Saturday, perhaps the start of the Annapolis–Newport Race. Early
in the week his boat captains arrive in Annapolis to
make sure the boat will be absolutely ready to go. All
the gear is inspected, sails are checked, the boat cleaned,
provisions laid in. As the crew arrives they turn to
and help.

The object of this whole exercise is called, "Let's make
Ted happy." Everyone knows from bitter experience
about Turner's moods and his impatience. That week
could have seen him in Washington at a broadcasters'
convention, in London on some business deal, or practically anywhere. Typically, he arrives in Annapolis late
Friday night, having caught the last possible plane into
the area. Everyone knows he will turn up at the boat
very early in the morning, and the entire crew is there
waiting for him.

He is very tense and looks grim as he strides down
the dock, small seabag in hand and engineer's cap on
his head. "What's going on?" he demands as he climbs
over the rail and pitches the seabag into the cockpit. A
quick look below where the sailbags are stacked, ready
to go, and then on deck, where the sheets are led
through the blocks and the crew is sitting ready to cast
off, are all he needs. You can see the tension begin to
melt away. "Hi, Ted," someone says quietly. Under-
neath the moustache, a bit of a smile forms. "Well,
damnit," Turner says, "let's go. What are we waiting for?"

Once the race starts, Turner begins to settle down

and get into the flow of the crew. Familiar routine takes over. He is the skipper; reporting to him are the two watch captains. He will spend the first day of the race with each watch, determining which one is doing the better job, then spend more time with the one that seems to be lacking. No watch captain wants the skipper on his watch, so Turner, in effect, is forcing some competition between the two watches to keep the boat moving. Still, he is careful with the men, setting a four-on, four-off structure so that everyone has a chance to rest and establish a pattern that will carry them to the finish line without undue fatigue.

Turner's own pattern consists of popping up when he is below on a long ocean leg, sensing what the boat is doing, and then going down again if he is satisfied. He has the seafaring instincts of the single-handed ocean sailor; sound asleep below, he will awaken instantly when the boat seems stalled, or doesn't have the right angle of heel, or if there is too much noise on deck. Then he will appear in the cockpit to get his forces reorganized. He is always in control.

"Okay," he says to the helmsman, "let me take it for a while." After steering for a few minutes, he understands what is slowing the boat, issues a few commands, and returns the wheel, knowing that the helmsman will have watched him carefully. There is no threat to the helmsman's ego; you know you wouldn't be on the boat if you weren't good, and Turner simply is asserting his rights as skipper.

As the race progresses, Turner's No. 1 priority is to keep the boat moving, day or night. He orders the crew to concentrate on speed rather than pointing as high as possible when the boat is close-hauled. In the ocean the wind can shift every four hours or so, so the object is to keep to the course set by the navigator and aim for boat speed, especially at night, when everyone else tends to get soggy. Turner always will sail a couple of degrees low, allowing the sails to be freed slightly to keep the vessel moving through the waves.

Turner's other priority is to keep the crew fresh and interested. His technique is simple. Eight members of the crew are sitting on the windward rail during a long beat. Turner says, "Okay, Conn, go down and check the jib lead for me. Gary, go forward and put a light on the mast and see how we're doing on the halyard tension." Perhaps nothing will be changed, but Turner has achieved his objective of getting people out of the lethargy that comes with sailing a long stretch on the same course.

The lethargy comes to an abrupt halt when Turner takes the wheel. He constantly talks to the trimmers while making mental preparation for the next evolution. He senses that the wind is beginning to come aft. The heavy No. 1 is up, and the reacher, a larger, more loosely cut sail, might be next.

"The wind's coming aft," he says. "I want the reacher on top of the pile. Let's get the reacher sheets led." He is ahead of the next move, ready to change gears quickly as the wind veers. The wind doesn't veer but gets stronger, and the decision must be made whether to change down to the No. 2. To avoid a sail change, other skippers would say, "Let's hold on to the number one a little longer and see what happens."

Not Turner. He says, "We'll try the number two for a while and decide which one is better." After fifteen minutes he says, "Let's put the number one back up. It's better."

On a Turner boat, no one ever argues sail changes

with him, even during one of those incredible afternoons when you wonder whether you will make it to the end of the race. At noon the wind is light but building. By 1:00 P.M. it's still building, about fifteen knots across the deck, and you're changing headsails. By 4:00 P.M. the wind is blowing thirty-five and the crew has unpacked every headsail, put it up, taken it down, packed it, and put it below until you're sailing with a small jib. In between, the main has been shortened down to a triple reef, everyone has taken turns going below to change into seaboots and foul-weather gear, lifelines have been rigged, and you know you're in for a stormy night.

Turner, below, is at his best during bad weather. "There really isn't that much to ocean racing," he jokes as he and the navigator listen to an NOAA weather forecast. The boat, however, is organized for the storm, based on his standing orders. And the boat is strong, based on one of his principles: "I haven't allowed myself to get caught up in the craze for light boats," he once wrote. "When the wind starts to really come on it's better to be prepared than to have to go right to the edge. Once you've gotten down to your storm canvas, you may not be going very fast, but there is not much that can go wrong."

In the end, the boat gets through the storm all right (just as Turner got it through the 1979 Fastnet) in our fictional Annapolis–Newport race, takes line honors and first in class, and as it sails into Newport Harbor, Turner begins to fidget again. He is going to make an appearance at the trophy awards, then head for Newport's little airfield, where a chartered plane awaits him. The crew slowly begins cleaning up, sorting out personal gear, coiling and stowing lines, stacking sailbags. The captain makes notes on gear that needs to be repaired or replaced before the next race. "Let's go. Let's go," Turner says as the boat comes into the dock, fenders out and lines ready. Even before the docklines are cleated, Turner's seabag is on the dock. "Good goin'," guys," he says as he trots off. There are phone calls to make, people to see. The clock is ticking.

At Home with Ted and Jane

The clock ticks the fastest for Turner when he is in Atlanta dealing with his network, his sports teams, his potential acquisitions, his real estate, and more recently, the Goodwill Games, Turner's single-handed détente with the Soviet Union that is reputed to have cost him upward of twenty-six million dollars.

When I first went to Atlanta, after Christmas in 1977, he was living in a big house in a subdivision and driving a small Toyota. It was a quiet week in the holiday season, but not for Turner. There were lunches every day at which several sides of his business life were represented—network VPs, real-estate men, officials from the Hawks and the Braves. It was typical of Turner to deal with more than one topic at a time, to have three events booked simultaneously and speed from one to the other, to be juggling parts of his life in a way that is both frightening and fascinating. In Atlanta I began to understand what *Tenacious* meant to him, the place where he could hide out and concentrate on one subject, how to get from A to B in the fastest way possible.

Turner that week was motion and impatience. I remember meeting his wife, Jane, and children who were home from school, and there were some evenings when he had his shoes off and his feet up, but most of the time remains a blur of Hawks games and meetings and driving around Atlanta.

Since 1977 Turner has moved out of the subdivision, making his home in one of the several establishments he owns in South Carolina, Georgia, and more recently near Tallahassee, Florida.. His properties include a home and an island off the South Carolina coast; a home on ninety acres outside Atlanta; a six-hundred-acre property in Buchanan, Ga.; a five-thousand-acre plantation near Tallahassee; and two plantations in South Carolina, one of twenty-six hundred acres and the other, not far away in Jacksonboro, of eight thousand acres.

The Jacksonboro place is called Hope Plantation and it's where I visited him not long ago. At the airport Jimmy Brown, Turner's family retainer of some thirty years, was waiting for me in an elderly station wagon. We drove for a few miles, then turned into a private road that continued across the fields. Deep in a grove of old shade trees stood the manor house with white pillars under a marble portico. On the steps stood Turner, wearing a white cowboy hat. And flowing out of the open front doorway was music—the score from *Gone with the Wind*.

Jane was there, too, a gracious hostess in the southern tradition. Inside, the first impression is of quiet because of the use of dark woods in the floors and wall moldings and the traditional walnut furniture. The interior is pure Americana, the kind of decor you are liable to see in many homes in New England. Yet there is something of the grandeur of the antebellum South in the house as well—a sweeping staircase to the second floor, high ceilings, bedrooms with old-fashioned four-poster bedsteads, and floor-to-ceiling windows.

The most popular room in the house is Turner's version of what is generally called "the family room." To the right of the entrance hall, it contains Turner's enormous collection of videofilms, comfortably upholstered sofas and chairs, and a huge stone fireplace that runs along the outside wall.

Turner has commissioned a number of striking paintings about the sea, and they are everywhere. There is his old ex-twelve, *American Eagle,* at Fastnet Rock and a remarkable one of *Courageous* and *Australia* in combat during the 1977 America's Cup, both painted by the distinguished marine artist John Mecray.

The second most popular room in the house is the dining room, with its fireplace and glass-fronted cabinets displaying silver and tableware and a long maple table that can seat a dinner party of twelve comfortably.

At the back of the house is a kitchen with all of the modern amenities—restaurant-type stove and refrigerator and leading-edge kitchen appliances. And at the rear entrance are a pair of mud rooms for putting away hunting and fishing clothing and boots and for storing guns.

There are three bedrooms on the second floor, but the Turners' master bedroom is on the first floor next to a small guest room. The house is situated so that the bedrooms are lit by the morning sun. When you wake up, the first thing you see outside is the two-acre pond that lies within a hundred yards of the house.

At Hope Plantation, Turner showed me a new side, the landed gentry at home. His impatience was dissipated, although the day's schedule had been laid out the night before. A typical day on the plantation proceeded something like this:

Wake-up call, 5:00 A.M. Deer-hunting for two hours (or duck-hunting, depending upon the season).

Return to the house at nine-thirty. Buffet breakfast prepared by the cook, another family retainer. Biscuits, ham, eggs, fruit. Lots of coffee.

About a half hour after breakfast, quail shooting in the woods. Return for lunch. Another spread.

In the afternoon, depart with Turner in the jeep for a dove-hunt or a pig-shoot. Some of the local people, mostly black, are there to help out. They don't tip their hats. They seem to like Turner, who has put some money into developing tree farms in the area.

In the late afternoon, the guns are stowed in the jeep and Turner drives around the plantation, just checking things out. He might look at his pet cougar, which lives in a fenced-in area that encompasses about an acre of land. He might drive to Kinloch, his other South Carolina plantation, about seventy miles away.

Then home. A quiet dinner around a sumptuously set dining-room table. Movies afterward, an old World War II film or a rerun of *Gone with the Wind*. An early evening. In the morning I leave for Annapolis, Turner for Atlanta, and Jane remains at Hope Plantation.

WALTER CRONKITE:
To Be Young Again

Sailing always has been stereotyped as a sport of the rich, which, of course, isn't really true anymore. Thousands of Americans sail or race for recreation without benefit of an overstuffed wallet or family inheritance. Not that sailing is inexpensive, as a trip to your local chandlery for a gallon of bottom paint will tell you.

But now something new is in the wind. Sailing has been discovered by the world of public relations as a fine way of publicizing people, places, and products. Sometimes it also promotes the sport. The latest phenomenon is the Celebrity Regatta, and it works like this:

Everyone wants to read about the rich and famous, so you gather as many of them as you can, put them in suitable boats with suitable coaches, and have them race each other. You load the cast with TV personalities, rock musicians, athletes, and a bona fide movie star or two, a sort of waterborne *People* magazine. The Celebrity Regatta makes for instant headlines and TV coverage, a lot more than you'll get from your local Sheepshead Bay Race Week, which might merit three paragraphs in a remote corner of the sports section.

In June 1986 in New York Harbor I participated in a Celebrity Regatta whose major aim was to promote the Liberty Cup that followed as well as be a forerunner of the July 4 Liberty weekend. Like the Liberty Cup, the race was run in French-manufactured Beneteau sloops, and the participants included a major movie star, Cliff Robertson, who disappeared in a limousine after the event; two members of the cast of *Miami Vice*; TV reporter Geraldo Rivera; and the Chicago Bears' incredible pass-catching end Wimmy Gault. I was in Gault's boat and it doesn't matter what the results were other than that everyone seemed to be having a good time and the press and TV coverage was remarkable. The *New York Post* ran a full-page story; the local TV stations had a field day with an event that allowed the newscasters to take a welcome break from the daily menu of crime and politics. The organizers topped the day off with a glittering party that made the society columns. In the end it seemed to me that despite the glitz, the sport of sailing suddenly had been glamorized, and that could only help increase interest.

The purists will argue that Celebrity Regattas focus attention in the wrong place—not on the race itself and what it takes to win it, but on the personalities involved. The celebrities become more important than the event, they say.

In reality, people of prominence always have been involved with boats, not necessarily to flaunt wealth or position. For instance, Thomas J. Watson, Jr., retired chairman of IBM, for many years raced a series of boats named *Palawan,* then had a sixty-five-footer built that he took to the Arctic and Antarctic on several exploratory voyages. A veteran airman (pilot for the inspector general of the U.S. Air Force in World War II), he was also very comfortable at sea, and not long ago, in the seventies, single-handed his latest *Palawan,* a forty-eight-foot sloop, from Antigua to Bermuda, much to the consternation of colleagues and family, "just to see if I could do it."

Sailing demands single-mindedness and concentration. If you are on the road, figuratively, constantly moving from one project to another, sailing provides the escape valve and the quiet thinking time to refresh creative energies and the spirit. Folk-rock singer Jimmy Buffett, who has been involved with boats since he was very young, keeps *Savannah Jane,* a twenty-eight-foot Nat Herreshoff-designed Alerion sloop, not far from his house in Key West. No engines for him. Only pure sailing will do as he takes *Savannah Jane* out into the

Gulf of Mexico between concert dates and recording sessions.

For many stars like Buffett (the Australians call them "identities"), the fact that they sail is not well known. It is, for some of them, a very private part of their lives. But it also says something about their sensibilities. The sea sets its own standards. No matter what you are onshore, at sea we are all alike, subject to the imposition of waves and weather. When the maxi Whitbread racer *Drum* overturned during the 1985 Fastnet race with its owner, rock star Simon Le Bon, on board, as far as the sea was concerned he was simply another intruder in its waters. As far as the sport of sailing was concerned, however, his participation gave more publicity to the Whitbread Round the World Race than it had had since its inception in 1975.

The list of those "identities" who sail is fascinating because it covers a wide range of people in the public eye. The common bond among them is their love for sailing and the sea; if there is any other link, we will leave it up to the reader to decide. Here are just a few:

Musicians:

Neil Young owns a famous schooner-rigged Baltic Trader of some eighty feet in length, the *J. R. Ragland,* which he has equipped with a small studio and extensive stereo equipment. Gordon Lightfoot owned a custom forty-three-foot sloop that he raced in the Great Lakes. Jimmy Buffett has had several boats. The most recent is the twenty-eight-foot Alerion sloop mentioned earlier.

Authors:

Novelist John Barth sails extensively in Chesapeake Bay and charters in the Caribbean. John D. McDonald, creator of "salvage expert" Travis McGee, owns a small powerboat and charters sailboats. Donald Hamilton, creator of detective Matt Helm, has sailed both coasts of the United States in his twenty-eight-foot sloop *Kathleen*. Stuart Woods, author of *Chiefs* and other novels, has sailed in the Observer Single-handed Transatlantic Race. William F. Buckley, Jr.'s, penchant for yachting has been memorialized in *Airborne*. British mystery writer Hammond Innes for years sailed small craft in and around England. Jonathan Raban, also British and author of the recently published *Foreign Land,* lives aboard his boat on the Cornish coast part of the time.

Hollywood:

Actor James Arness teamed up with his catamaran *Sea Smoke* to win the Multihull TransPac. So did Buddy Ebsen with *Polynesian Concept,* a catamaran that broke through the speed barrier in TransPac racing. Screenwriter Stirling Silliphant (*In the Heat of the Night*) owned a seventy-six-foot Swan ketch on which he was based for some time. (In two new novels, his hero, John Locke, ex-cop and Green Beret, lives aboard a Swan in southeastern Pacific waters and "solves problems" of a violent nature for clients.)

Sailboats played a big role in some past Hollywood lives. Well known was Humphrey Bogart's big ketch, *Santana,* and infamous was Errol Flynn's *Sirocco,* which became his sexual playpen.

Politicians:

Former British Prime Minister Edward Heath owned several ocean racers named *Morning Cloud* and was a member of the British Admiral's Cup team. Jimmy Carter takes time away from Plains, Ga., to sail aboard his twenty-three-foot sloop off St. Simons Island, Ga.

Royalty:

Prince Charles is an active sailor who races small and

large boats competitively. His father, Prince Philip, also
a small–boat sailor, was a companion of British yacht
designer Uffa Fox and often raced Flying Fifteens with
him. King Juan Carlos of Spain and Prince Olav of
Norway skippered Dragons in the Olympics.

Broadcasting:

Robert MacNeil, coanchorman of the PBS news
program *The MacNeil-Lehrer Report,* sails his own vessel
in Chesapeake Bay. And Walter Cronkite is a sailing
man with a close, long–standing relationship with
the sea.

Cronkite, as everyone knows, has retired from *The
CBS Evening News,* but he has not retired from his other
love, sailing. He spends his summers at his wide–ver-
andaed house overlooking Edgartown Harbor on Mar-
tha's Vineyard with his new forty–eight–foot yacht
moored in the harbor below among the gold–platers of
the Edgartown Yacht Club fleet. During the winter
when not working (he still does special assignments for
CBS News) you may find him somewhere along the
Intracoastal Waterway, a body of water he is particularly fond of and has written about. Residents along
the waterway, which stretches from New Jersey to
Texas, return that fondness with stories of their own.
A lady who is in charge of the bridge over the Neuse
River in New Bern, N.C., remembers Cronkite well.
One year he went hard aground near the bridge in his
Westsail 42, *Wyntje,* and as she told it, "He was stuck
for two days. Nothing ever happens in New Bern, you
understand. So everyone from miles around came down
to see Walter hard aground. Biggest traffic jam we ever
had in this county."

Later he wrote in the *Waterway Guide,* which lists

him on the masthead as editorial consultant, " 'What do I do if' . . . should be the question foremost in mind. An awful lot of trouble can be avoided if the helmsman is thinking and weighing the variables that could affect the boat in the minutes and hours ahead."

One of his favorite stops is Annapolis, where he may be seen in October around the sailboat show or in McGarvey's Restaurant, where owner Mike Ashford has named a special fish Captain Cronkite's Steak in his honor.

I had met Captain Cronkite in 1977 aboard *Courageous* when he had come to Newport to do a documentary report on the America's Cup. I remembered liking him for his cheerfulness and that, for all of his seriousness on the air, he was not terribly impressed with himself. But he knew how to do his job, how to keep his feet under him on *Courageous,* and how to bring off an interesting interview with the three American skippers, Turner, North, and Hood, without interposing himself. He sailed on *Courageous* and was intrigued by the boat and the crew. Once while the boat was reaching off at speed he said to Turner, "How about letting me steer for a while," to which Turner replied, "I'll let you steer if you let me do the evening news."

It was Mike Ashford who asked me if I'd like to sail to Bermuda with Cronkite and him and some CBS sailors on *Wyntje* in the 1981 Marion–Bermuda Race. The race is strictly for cruising-type vessels that are not designed exclusively for speed; spinnakers are eschewed. I knew it would be slow, especially aboard Cronkite's Westsail, a deep, tubby boat modeled after certain Colin Archer-designed North Sea fishing vessels made for staying put in heavy seas rather than speeding over the waves. But the prospect of sailing with "the most trusted man in America" (according to opinion polls) was intriguing. Cronkite at that time was entertaining the idea of doing some world cruising, and he thought that the Marion–Bermuda affair would give him some idea of what blue-water voyaging might be like.

The 645-mile race started on June 19 from Marion, Mass., on Buzzard's Bay, and ended for us becalmed off Bermuda 6½ days later in one of the slowest passages between the two points that had ever been raced. In between, we had the typical Gulf Stream conditions—fog, heavy squalls, some pleasant sailing, and finally no wind. There was even some controversy before the start of the race. Some of the organizers were unhappy that Cronkite had entered the race, fearing that he rather than the event would catch the press, a rather shortsighted view if there ever was one. They were not happy about my being aboard, either, feeling that Cronkite was getting professional help. In the end, however, it didn't matter; we wound up motoring into St. George's after being becalmed for thirty-six hours.

If there was any help that could be called professional given on board, it was during one critical period when the genoa blew apart in the face of an oncoming squall. The wind was building to forty-five knots when the sail split in half. With the halyard jammed at the masthead, it was impossible to get the sail down the luff track on the forestay; there was nothing to do but for someone to be hauled to the top of the mast and free the halyard. It was a very unpleasant experience with the wind gusting and tearing at my body while I sat in the bosun's chair and tried to hold on to the mast with one hand while getting at the halyard shackle, which had jammed in the masthead sheave, with the other. Finally, when the halyard was free, I looked down to find all of the crew, including Cronkite, taking pictures of me. He yelled, "You can come down now, Gary, your watch is over!"

Cronkite had fitted out *Wyntje* well. She was a comfortable, deep boat with plenty of headroom, an all-teak interior with traditional sea berths. A good seaman, he had written out detailed instructions for everything on board and kept a stowage plan, like a chart, that showed the position of all of the gear and provisions. Like all good skippers he had held a briefing session well before the start and was very clear on how he expected the boat to be run.

On deck, Cronkite proved tough. At sixty-five, he loved to steer and stood his full watch at the helm. Unfortunately, it was one of those crossings to Bermuda when you are hard on the wind most of the time. Close-hauled, *Wyntje*'s best speed was about 5½ knots, with a tendency to make about ten degrees of leeway. But the skipper was unflappable about the lack of speed. When the weather was good and he was off watch, he would settle back in the cockpit in the afternoon with a can of Rolling Rock Beer and talk about his life as a newsman, with stories ranging from covering the Nuremberg trials, where he interviewed Hermann Goering, to getting out of Saigon at the end of the Vietnam War.

It was all very casual. It was very easy to forget that the man with the familiar lined face and that amused smile sitting across from you in the cockpit was one of the most experienced newsmen in America, an observer of world events since the days of Edward R. Murrow. Here was CRONKITE, for God's sake, who had anchored all of those presidential nominating conventions and who had described all of the space shoots since the program began, a friend of all of the astronauts and an interviewer of heads of state. Now that well-known voice was heard to call below for another Rolling Rock. It was exceptional.

Once you got past that feeling, it was the voice of a skipper talking to you as well. Once, when another squall was imminent and I leaped for the jib halyard to get the genoa down and yelled for one of the crew to go forward and take in the sail, he said to me quietly, "Gary, why don't you just roll it up?" I realized with embarrassment that for the first time in my career I was racing with a roller furling jib. Then he said, "You sure can move fast. I would give anything to be your age again."

SAM MERRICK:
Tiller, Telephone, and Pen

In 1939, Sam Merrick, a twenty-six-year-old athlete who stood six-three in his wool socks, won the E-scow Easterns. Twenty-eight years later, in 1967, with a lanky Barnegat Bay junior sailing instructor as crew, he again won the E-scow Easterns. In 1984, at age 71, he pulled off a coup at the summer Olympics that never had been achieved by an American sailing team. As director of the Olympic sailing program, his sailors had swept every class, picking up three gold and four silver medals in the seven Olympic classes. Later that year Merrick was awarded the Nathaniel G. Herreshoff Trophy, given annually by the U.S. Yacht Racing Union (the parent body of organized sailing) for "the individual who has made the most outstanding contribution to the sport."

Merrick, about to retire as an attorney and lobbyist in Washington, had a national reputation as a foremost one-design racer when he was selected to become a director of the USYRU Olympic Yachting Committee. The American Olympic sailing effort was a piecemeal operation in those days, without the kind of organized effort that characterized the strong European teams the Americans raced against. There had been a number of individual medalists over the years, but Merrick had something else in mind—to win as many medals as possible in each of the seven Olympic events; in effect, to sweep the Olympics.

Between 1977 and 1979, in preparation for the 1980 Summer Games in Moscow (the yachting events were to be held in Tallinn, Estonia), Merrick began a scheme to get the country's top racers into the Olympic ranks. He and I ranged the country, appearing at yacht clubs where clinics were held in Olympic classes such as Stars, Finns, and Solings. Then, in an unprecedented move, Merrick appealed to racers in the non-Olympic classes to try out for one of the Olympic events.

The most challenging clinic I ran during that period was prior to a Star regatta at the New Orleans Yacht Club in New Orleans. Among the attendees at the clinic were Bill Buchan, Tom Blackaller, John Dane, and Peter Wright, all champions. What could I, who had very little experience in Stars, tell them that they didn't already know? Instead I organized drills and short-course races of the type I had used when coaching, which turned out to be very helpful in sharpening skills.

The 1980 effort ended in frustration and disappointment for American athletes, including the yachting community, which had been looking forward to sending a strong team to Tallinn, when the U.S. government pulled out of the Olympic Games in protest against the Soviet invasion of Afghanistan. But the cancellation didn't stop Merrick, who had become chairman of the Olympic Yachting Committee and in a better position to have his way.

His way was to concentrate on a few sailors who had proven themselves capable of winning and get them to compete in the Olympic classes. To do this he set up a national ranking system. The skippers and crews of the top six boats in each class were selected in national trials and then brought to Long Beach, Calif., for training under team coach Robert Hopkins. The Merrick system was not without controversy. While it focused, in the end, on a few dozen racers, it also had the effect of discouraging Olympic hopefuls from trying out because suddenly they found that the top spots in their classes had been filled by champions and near-champions from non-Olympic classes who had been recruited because of their sailing abilities.

Whatever the means, Merrick's system worked. At Long Beach in 1984, the Olympic yachting team garnered more golds and silvers than any of the other American teams, but you never would have known it from the TV coverage, which seemed more concerned with water ballet than with the excitement of close-fought dinghy racing among the finest one-design sailors in the world.

Merrick, typically, played down his role in achieving this extraordinary success. All he did was develop the talent, advance the technology, pick up the pieces after the 1980 debacle, lobby for funding from USYRU, stretch the dollars, plan the trials, recruit the support staff and coaches, and motivate the sailors. "After that," he said, "there was nothing to do but applaud."

The members of USYRU thought otherwise. At the awards ceremony it was stated, "He is equally adept with a tiller, a telephone, and a pen. He prepared an outstanding team for the 1980 Olympics only to be frustrated by the boycott. After that, to build a record-breaking team took inspiration, leadership, and plain seven-days-a-week hard work."

Merrick, for his part, was not convinced. In accepting the trophy he said, "In honoring me you honor the team and also those fine sailors who missed by inches."

The following weekend saw Merrick out on Chesapeake Bay, competing in the Severn Racing Association's frostbite series as if nothing had ever happened. The only connection one might find with the Olympics was his Soling. But there were lots of them out there.

Merrick, now seventy-three, still races in Annapolis waters during the winter and in Barnegat Bay during the summer, as he has done for most of his adult life. I still crew for him occasionally in the winter frostbite fleet aboard his Soling, just as I did on his E-scow twenty years ago. Our relationship has changed from avuncular adult-adolescent to two adults who meet as friends in Washington, D.C., each month for lunch and a good talk. I still seek his counsel, as I learned to do when we raced together on Barnegat Bay.

In those days, advice was not easily forthcoming. Nor was it eagarly sought by the teenager. In 1966, not only had I achieved success as a junior racer but also had been hired as an instructor in the junior program at the

Toms River Yacht Club, one of the oldest on the bay. For someone who had grown up in the not very posh quarters of the Beachwood Yacht Club, this was quite an upward move, I thought, and it stretched my self-confidence to the breaking point.

Merrick, when he invited me to sail with him, had a lot to do with my development by treating me not as a kid but as a fellow sailor. I could be trusted to treat his boat with the same respect he did. When he sailed, a relationship of equality developed on the boat in discussing tactics and keeping track of wind shifts and courses. I learned, too, about sail testing and gear testing and the extra effort he always put into sailing his boats. He was not a natural sailor. Everything he knew about racing he had learned from books and from trial and error on the water, including the adoption of the Buddy Melges technique of playing wind shifts downwind, jibing to get high angles.

Off the boat we talked about our favorite sailing books, and he was interested in what I had to say and what plans I was making for the future. We finally reached a point where I felt I could talk to him about myself and he could tell me about his career in Washington, which had begun during the Roosevelt administration as an attorney in the Department of Commerce.

So began a mentor relationship with Sam Merrick that has lasted almost two decades. In 1967, when we won the E-scows Easterns, neither of us could have predicted that we would be frostbiting aboard a Soling together on the Severn River twenty years later. Sam Merrick is forty years older than I, but we have a common denominator: We love to race. Especially with each other.

JOE PROSSER:
Sailing Master

Captain Charles Arthur Prosser, known as "Joe" to his friends and "Captain" to the hundreds of midshipmen who passed through his hands at the U.S. Merchant Marine Academy, died at Kings Point, N.Y., in April 1986 while this book was being written. His death was a heavy personal loss for me because he had been a mentor during an important period of my life and remained a friend until his death.

It was Prosser who taught me the most about coaching. What I know now about the care and feeding of young racers I learned in the four years I spent under him as coach of the Kings Point sailing team.

Our relationship began from afar. As a member of the sailing team of the New York Maritime College, much of our impromptu racing was held with the Kings Point sailors across Long Island Sound from us. It was impossible to avoid Prosser; a burly, overweight man with a face that seemed to be in a permanent growl, he worked very closely with his team and wasn't shy about yelling at the sailors from New York Maritime, perhaps because we were all training for the same jobs at sea and he felt there was a common bond.

We had our battles on the water, but I admired his ability to handle his crews and felt that he was a true three-dimensional character; obviously there was more to him than just a pudgy body in foul-weather gear. I wrote to him and applied for a coach's job; I knew there would be a vacancy, and in the spring of 1973 he hired me to cross over to Kings Point after I graduated.

I accepted, telling him earnestly that I would continue sailing for Fort Schuyler until the end of the school year and that Kings Point could expect no quarter from me.

"I wouldn't expect anything else, my son," he said as we shook hands.

I learned the following fall that Captain Prosser always addressed you as "my son" and that that was only one of the whimsical, surprising things about him. He was from Newfoundland of English descent and had been well educated in England. "I'm a goofy Newfie" is the way he described himself in his usual self-deprecating style, "weaned on clambakes, schooners, and rum."

Soon you discovered that his rank of captain was not just a title you lay on someone who is a skipper. Prosser had earned his rank the hard way during the Second World War as an officer in the Canadian Navy. He had been given his first command at twenty-seven, had been torpedoed by a German U-boat, so the story went, and had escaped from a POW compound by garroting a guard with piano wire.

Prosser had wound up at Kings Point through a friend who knew that the twelve-meter *Weatherly* was to be at the Academy during the summer of 1966 and needed a sailing master. Prosser took over the job. Then in 1967 he joined the Academy as sailing master, having convinced the superintendent that he could give the school a winning sailing team. He also applied for American citizenship so he could be a government employee—a "snivel servant," as he called it.

He had his own terms for everything. He referred to his liquor as "mother's milk" and his bachelor apartment above the superintendent's garage as "Codfish Manor." (A marriage in Canada had failed when his wife disappeared along with their four children.) His apartment was noted for its collection of frog ceramics, mugs, and other *objets d'art*. "What is it with the frogs?" I once asked. "It's because I look like a frog," he answered. Every day for the four years I was with him he wore red and green socks, apparently to remind his sailors about port (red) and starboard (green).

I spent many hours with Prosser on the water, where he was a surprisingly good sailor considering his bulk; in his office, where one chair, the "hot seat," was painted red; and evenings in Codfish Manor, where he was an impeccable host. He was the most generous of men. If you said, "Captain, I need a hundred dollars and the keys to your car," he wouldn't think twice about it— just reach for his wallet and his keys.

Much of what I learned from Prosser was in his office, where he would quietly go about running the team and using the "hot seat" to discipline members of the team who had gone astray. In one instance, a member of the team who had been incensed over something wrote Prosser a nasty letter. Prosser said nothing about it for three weeks while the midshipman became more and more uncomfortable every time they saw each other. One day the captain called the young sailor to his office, beckoned him to the red chair, and continued with his work. Finally he turned to the midshipman and said, "Son, next time you write a letter like that, sit on it for twenty-four hours before you mail it. You can go now."

Prosser taught me about the importance of correspondence and staying in touch with other college coaches and regatta chairmen. He taught me how to organize training schedules and set up drills on the water. His method of coaching was through repeating a technique until it becomes second nature. I learned from him that a large percentage of building a good college sailing program was through recruitment.

Joe Prosser worked every day of his life. If he wasn't busy with the sailing team, he would be involved with some project for the American Sail Training Association. He would fit it in between going on trips with us; he was known everywhere and welcomed at college and yacht club regattas. He became a member of the New York Yacht Club in 1951, and he was equally comfortable in the hallowed halls of Oyster Bay's *Seawanhaka* as in a college cafeteria.

Yet that sense of humor was irrepressible. When Janice and I were married in 1974, he came to the wedding at Kings Point resplendent in the whitest of white suits, looking like a very large reincarnation of the Godfather. One winter Sunday, with snow whipping across the streets of Great Neck, L.I., where we lived, a big Cadillac wheeled up to the door at 8:30 A.M. The first sounds we heard were the blasts of air horns, the kind used by boatmen to signal bridge tenders. We leaped out of bed and there, standing at the door, were Joe Prosser and his girlfriend wearing red nightshirts and yellow foul-weather gear.

"Looks like a boring Sunday," he said, "so we thought we'd see what you were up to."

In September 1984, a testimonial dinner was given at Kings Point to honor Prosser. I was racing in the Big Boat Series in San Francisco at the time, but there was no way I was going to miss the affair for Prosser. I left San Francisco early in the morning and flew to New York, arriving at the dinner about thirty minutes before it started. Friends and colleagues were there from the Naval and Merchant Marine academies, college sailing teams, the American Sail Training Association, and the yachting community, and many ex-midshipmen who had come under his influence. The following morning I flew back to the West Coast, saddened to have learned that Prosser had contracted cancer.

There was no stopping Prosser, however. He kept working as he always did, and when he died at sixty-seven it was of a heart attack. The chronometer of the "goofy Newfie" had simply run down.

Afterword:
Kristi and the Fish Sun

*W*hen my human alarm clock, 2½-year-old Kristi, woke me at 6:30 A.M. one Saturday morning, she didn't, as usual, want to have a book read to her. She wanted to play a game, and I had just the game for her.

By 8:30 A.M. we were ready to sail our Sunfish on Spa Creek. It was Kristi's first sail on our little boat, probably the best craft of all for beginning sailors. A Sunfish is a little bit less than fourteen feet long, about four feet wide, and draws about two inches of water with the centerboard up and two feet, seven inches with the board down. Kristi had been taking swimming lessons, and when we got to the dock the hardest problem was keeping her from jumping in.

With the boat alongside the dock, I put Kristi into her life jacket and then got the Sunfish ready to sail. "All set, Kristi?" I asked her. "Where is your life jacket,

Daddy?'' she answered with perfect logic.

I had three things in mind to teach Kristi in our first session. First was that the boat can heel. Second was that when I said "ready about" we were going to change sides and that when I said "jibe" she was to put her head down.

We sailed out into the stream. It was early and we had the creek to ourselves. The breeze was just enough to move the Sunfish along. Kristi particularly liked tacking. It was fun moving from side to side, and she was small enough to stand up without hitting her head on the bottom of the boom. When we jibed it took a little extra coaching to get her to lift her head back up after the boom had passed over. When we heeled, she kept diving to leeward to put her hands in the water. She didn't comprehend that dragging her feet or hands overboard would slow the boat down. Against all of my racing instincts I said nothing.

As we passed dozens of moored boats in the creek, she asked alertly, "Where are all the people, Daddy?" Then she said, "Sooo many boats."

She particularly liked the ducks we chased from one end of the creek to the other. They would rise out of the water, fly a short distance, and then settle down in the water again. Kristi called them. "Quack, quack," she said.

Then we sailed by some rowboats, the water hissing under our bow. Kristi sang, "Row, row, row, row, down the stream."

We came about and headed back and Kristi sat quietly, taking it all in. I said, "We're going home now, Kristi." She didn't complain. "Okay, Daddy," she said, and I thought, Had we done too much? Was she still interested?

At home she said very little about the sail, even when Janice pressed her. "Maybe she's too young," I said to Janice.

On Sunday afternoon I could see ripples in the water from our back windows. The weather was clear. Kristi had been playing in her room and I was working at the kitchen table when she came to me. "Fish sun, Daddy," she said. "Fish sun?" It took me a minute to understand her name for our sailboat. Then I said, "Okay, Kristi, get your life vest."

We went down to the dock once again, rigged the Sunfish, and set sail. This time, without hesitation, Kristi decided it was time she should steer. I gave her the tiller and she wiggled it back and forth, laughing every time the boat changed course. After our first outing she obviously had thought about it and decided that she really liked sailing and she especially liked making the boat wiggle. "Fun, Daddy," she said. "Fun fish."

Kristi has sailed on the Sunfish quite a bit with me since then. She dangles her feet in the water and she splashes and sometimes she asks to steer, and each time she does, the boat wiggles a little bit less. One day she will learn that there is a world beyond Spa Creek, just as I learned that there was a world beyond Toms River. But for now it doesn't matter. The Fish sun is enough.